I0055458

THE

ELEMENTS OF THE COMMON LAWES OF ENGLAND,

Branched into a double Tract:

THE ONE

Contayning a Collection of some principall Rules and Maximes of the Common Law, with their Latitude and Extent.

Explicated for the more facile Introduction of such as are studiously addicted to that noble Profession.

THE OTHER

The Use of the Common Law, for preseruation of our Persons, Goods, and good Names.

According to the Lawes and Customes of this Land.

By the late Sir *Francis Bacon* Knight, Lo: Verulam and Viscount S. Alban.

Videre Vtilitas.

THE LAWBOOK EXCHANGE, LTD.
Clark, New Jersey

ISBN 978-1-58477-248-4

Lawbook Exchange edition 2003, 2019

The quality of this reprint is equivalent to the quality of the original work.

THE LAWBOOK EXCHANGE, LTD.
33 Terminal Avenue
Clark, New Jersey 07066-1321

Please see our website for a selection of our other publications and fine facsimile reprints of classic works of legal history:
www.lawbookexchange.com

Library of Congress Cataloging-in-Publication Data

Bacon, Francis, 1561-1626.
The elements of the common lawes of England / by Sir Francis Bacon.
p.cm.
"Branched into a double tract : the one, contayning a collection of some principall rules and maximes of the common law, with their latitude and extent explicated for the more facile introduction of such as are studiously addicted to that noble profession: the other, the use of the common law for preservation of our persons, goods, and good names, according to the lawes and customes of this land."
Originally published: London : Assignes of I. More, 1630.
Includes bibliographical references.
ISBN 1-58477-248-4 (cloth: alk. paper)
1. Law—Great Britain. 2. Legal maxims—Great Britain. I. Title.

KD600 .B3 2002
349.42—dc2l 2002025942

Printed in the United States of America on acid-free paper

THE

ELEMENTS OF THE COMMON LAWES OF ENGLAND,

Branched into a double Tract:

THE ONE

Contayning a Collection of some principall Rules and Maximes of the Common Law, with their Latitude and Extent.

Explicated for the more facile Introduction of such as are studiously addicted to that noble Profession.

THE OTHER

The Use of the Common Law, for preservation of our Persons, Goods, and good Names.

According to the Lawes and Customes of this Land.

By the late Sir *Francis Bacon* Knight, Lo: Verulam and Viscount S. Alban.

Videre Utilitas.

LONDON,
Printed by the Assignes of *I. More* Esq. 1630.

A COLLECTION OF SOME PRINCIPALL RVLES and MAXIMES of the Common Lawes of ENGLAND, WITH THEIR LATITVDE and EXTENT,

Explicated for the more facile Introduction of ſuch as are ſtudiouſly addicted to that noble Profeſsion.

By Sir FRANCIS BACON, then Sollicitor *generall to the late renowned Queene* Elizabeth, *and ſince Lord Chancellor of* ENGLAND.

Orbe paruo ſed non occiduo.

LONDON,
Printed by the Aſsignes of *Iohn Moore* Eſq.
Anno cIↃ.IↃ.C.XXX.

CVM PRIVILEGIO.

TO HER SACRED MAIESTY.

Doe here most humbly present and dedicate vnto your Sacred Maiesty a sheife and cluster of fruit, of the good and fauourable season, which by the influence of your happy gouernment wee enioy; for if it be true, that silent leges inter arma, *it is also as true, that your Maiesty is in a double respect the life of our lawes: Once, because without your authority they are but* litera mortua, *and againe, because you are the life of our peace, without which lawes are put to silence; and as the vitall spirits doe not onely maintaine and moue the body, but also contend to perfect and renew it, so your Sacred Maiesty, who is* anima legis, *doth not only giue vnto your lawes force and vigour, but also hath bin*

carefull of their amendment and reforming; where-in your Maiesties proceeding may be compared as in that part of your gouernment (for if your gouernment bee considered in all the parts, it is incomparable) with the former doings of the most excellent Princes that euer haue reigned, whose study altogether hath beene alwaies to adorne and honour times of peace, with the amendment of the policy of their lawes. Of this proceeding in Augustus Cæsar, *the testimony yet remaines.*

Pace data terris animum ad ciuilia vertit
Iura suum, legesq; tulit iustissimus auctor.

Hence was collected the difference betweene gesta in armis *and* acta in toga, *whereof he disputeth thus.*

Ecquid est quod tam proprie dici potest, actum eius qui togatus in republica cum potestate imperioq; versatus sit, quam lex? quære acta Gracchi? leges Sempronij proferantur, quære Sillæ Corneliæ? quid Cn. Pom. tertius consulatus in quibus actis consistet? nempe, in legibus: à Cæsare ipso si quæreres quidnam egisset in vrbe, & toga leges multas se responderet & præclaras tulisse.

The same desire long after did spring in the Emperor Iustinian, being rightly called, Vltimus Imperatorum Romanorum, *who hauing peace in the heart of his Empire, and making his warres prosperously in the remote places of his dominions by his liuetenants, chose it for a monument and honour of his gouernment, to reuise the Romane lawes from infinite volumes, and much repugnancy, into one competent*

petent and uniforme corps of law; of which matter himselfe doth speake gloriously, and yet aptly calling of it, proprium & sanctissimum templum iustitiæ consecratum, *a worke of great excellency, indeed, as may well appeare in that France, Italy, & Spaine, which haue long since shaken off the yoke of the Romane Empire, doe yet neuerthelesse continue to vse the policy of that law: but more excellent had the worke beene, saue that the more ignorant, and obscure time vndertooke to correct the more learned and flourishing time. To conclude with the domesticall example of one of your Maiesties royall Ancestors; King Edward the first your Maiesties famous progenitor, and the principall Law-giuer of our nation, after hee had in his younger yeares giuen himselfe satisfaction in the glory of armes, by the enterprize of the holy land, and hauing inward peace, otherwise then for the inuasions which himselfe made vpon Wales and Scotland, parts farre distant from the Centre of the Realme, hee bent himselfe to endow his state with sundry notable and fundamentall lawes, vpon which the gouernment hath euer since principally rested: of this example, and others the like, two reasons may bee giuen; the one, because that Kings, which either by the moderation of their natures, or the maturity of their years and iudgement, do temper their magnanimity with iustice, do wisely consider & conceiue of the exploits of ambitious warres, as actions rather great than good, and so distasted with that course of winning honour, they conuert their mindes rather to doe somewhat for the better vniting of humane society, than for the dissoluing or disturbing of the same. Another reason is, because times of peace, for the most part drawing with them abundance of wealth, and finenesse of cunning, doe draw also in further consequence multitudes of suits, and controuersies, and abuses of law by euasions, and deuices; which inconueniencies in such time growing more generall, do more instantly sollicite for the amendment of lawes, to restraine and represse them.*

Your Maiesties reigne hauing beene blessed from the Highest with inward peace, and falling into an age wherein if science bee increased, conscience is rather decayed, and if mens wits bee great, their wills bee greater; and wherein also lawes are multiplied in number, and slackened in vigour and execution, It was not possible but that not onely suits in law should multiply and increase (whereof a great part are alwaies vniust) but also that all the indirect courses and practices to abuse law and iustice should haue bin much attempted and put in vre, which no doubt had bred greater enormities, had they not by the royall policy of your Maiesty, by the censure and fore-sight of your Councell table and Star-chamber, and by the grauity and integrity of your Benches beene repressed and restrained; for it may bee truly obserued, that as concerning frauds in contracts, bargaines and assurances, and abuses of lawes by delaies, couins, vexations, and corruptions in Informers, Iurors, Ministers of iustice, and the like; there haue beene sundry excellent statutes made in your Maiesties time, more in number, and more politique in prouision, than in any

your

your Maiesties predeceſſors times.

But I am an vnworthy witneſſe to your Maieſty, of an higher intention and proiect, both by that which was publiſhed by your Chancellor in full Parliament from your royall mouth, in the 35. *of your happie reigne; and much more by that which I haue beene ſince vouchſafed to vnderſtand from your Maieſtie, imparting a purpoſe for theſe many yeares, infuſed into your Maieſties breaſt, to enter into a generall amendment of the ſtates of your lawes, and to reduce them to more breuity and certaintie, that the great hollowneſſe and vnſafety in aſſurances of lands and goods may bee ſtrengthened, the ſwaruing penalties that lye vpon many ſubiects remoued, the execution of many profitable lawes reuiued, the Iudge better directed in his ſentence, the Counſellor better warranted in his counſaile, the Student eaſed in his reading, the contentious Suitor that ſeeketh but vexation diſarmed, and the honeſt Suitor that ſeeketh but to obtaine his right, relieued; which purpoſe and intention as it did ſtrike mee with great admiration, when I heard it, ſo it might bee acknowledged to bee one of the moſt choſen works, and of higheſt merit and beneficence towards the ſubiect that euer entred into the minde of any King; greater than wee can imagine, becauſe the imperfections and dangers of the lawes are couered vnder the clemency and excellent temper of your Maieſties gouernment. And though there bee rare preſidents of it in gouernment, as it commeth to paſſe in things ſo excellent, there being no preſident full in view but of* Iuſtinian, *yet I muſt ſay as* Cicero

ſaid

said to Cæsar, Nihil vulgatum te dignum videri potest; *and as it is no doubt a precious seed sowne in your Maiesties heart by the hand of Gods diuine Maiestie, so I hope in the maturity of your Maiesties owne time it will come vp and beare fruit. But to returne thence whither I haue beene carried, obseruing in your Maiesty, vpon so notable proofes and grounds, this disposition in generall of a prudent and royall regard to the amendment of your lawes, and hauing by my priuate labour and trauell collected many of the grounds of the common lawes, the better to establish and settle a certaine sense of law, which doth now too much wauer in incertaintie, I conceiued the nature of the subiect, besides my particular obligation, was such, as I ought not to dedicate the same to any other than to your sacred Maiestie; both because, though the collection bee mine, yet the lawes are yours; and because it is your Maiesties reigne that hath beene as a goodly seasonable spring-weather to the aduancing of all excelent arts of peace. And so concluding with a prayer answerable to the present argument, which is, That God will continue your Maiesties reigne in a happy and renowned peace, and that he will guide both your policy and armes to purchase the continuance of it with suerty and honour, I most humbly craue pardon, and commend your Maiestie to the diuine preseruation.*

Your sacred Maiesties most humble
and obedient subiect and seruant,

FRANCIS BACON.

The

THE PREFACE.

Hold euery man a debtor to his profeſſion, from the which, as men of courſe doe ſeeke to receiue countenance & profit, ſo ought they of duty to endeauour themſelues by way of amends to bee a helpe and ornament thereunto; this is performed in ſome degree, by the honeſt and liberall practice of a profeſſion, when men ſhall carry a reſpect not to deſcend into any courſe that is corrupt, and vnworthy thereof, and preſerue themſelues free from the abuſes wherewith the ſame profeſſion is noted to bee infected; but much more is this performed, if a man bee able to viſite and ſtrengthen the roots and foundation of the ſcience it ſelfe; thereby not onely gracing it in reputation and dignity, but alſo amplifying it in perfection and ſubſtance. Hauing therefore from

the beginning comne to the ſtudy of the lawes of this Realme, with a deſire no leſſe (if I could attaine vnto it) that the ſame lawes ſhould bee the better for my induſtry, than that my ſelfe ſhould bee the better for the knowledge of them; I doe not finde, that by mine owne trauell, without the helpe of authority, I can in any kinde conferre ſo profitable an addition vnto that ſcience, as by collecting the rules & grounds, diſperſed throughout the body of the ſame lawes; for hereby no ſmall light will bee giuen in new caſes, wherein the authorities doe ſquare and varie, to confirme the law, and to make it receiued one way, and in caſes wherein the law is cleered by authoritie; yet neuertheleſſe to ſee more profoundly into the reaſon of ſuch iudgements and ruled caſes, and thereby to make more vſe of them for the deciſion of other caſes more doubtfull; ſo that the incertainty of law, which is the principall and moſt iuſt challenge that is made to the lawes of our nation at this time, will, by this new ſtrength laid to the foundation, be ſomewhat the more ſettle and corrected; Neither will the vſe hereof be only in deciding of doubts, and helping ſoundneſſe of iudgement, but further in gracing of argument, in correcting vnprofitable ſubtilty, and reducing the ſame to a more ſound and ſubſtantiall ſenſe of law, in reclaiming vulgar errors, and generally the amendment in ſome meaſure of the very nature and complection of the whole law, and therfore

fore the conclusions of reason of this kinde are worthily and aptly called by a great Ciuilian *legum leges*, lawes of lawes, for that many *placita legum*, that is, particular and positiue learnings of lawes doe easily decline from a good temper of iustice, if they bee not rectified and gouerned by such rules.

Now for the manner of setting downe of them, I haue in all points to the best of my vnderstanding and fore-sight applied my selfe not to that which might seeme most for the ostentation of mine owne wit or knowledge, but to that which may yeeld most vse and profit to the Students and professors of our lawes.

And therefore, whereas these rules are some of them ordinary and vulgar, that now serue but for grounds and plaine songs to the more shallow and impertinent sort of arguments: other of them are gathered and extracted out of the harmony and congruity of cases, and are such as the wisest and deepest sort of Lawyers haue in iudgement, and vse, though they bee not able many times to expresse and set them downe.

For the former sort, which a man that should rather write to raise an high opinion of himselfe, than to instruct others, would haue omitted, as trite and within euery mans compasse; yet neuerthelesse I haue not affected to neglect them, but haue chosen out of them such as I thought good: I haue reduced them to a true application, limiting and defining their bounds,that they may not bee read vpon at large,but restrained to a point of difference; for as both in the law and other sciences the handling of questions by Commonplace without aime or application is the weakest, so yet neuerthelesse many common principles and generalities are not to bee contemned, if they bee well deriued and deduced into particulars, and their limits and exclusions duely assigned: for there bee two contrary faults and extremities in the debating and sifting out of the law, which may bee best noted in two seuerall manner of arguments: Some argue vpon generall grounds, and come not neere the point in question; others without laying any foundation of a ground or difference doe loosely put cases, which though they goe neere the point, yet being put so scattered, proue not, but rather serue to make the law appeare more doubtfull, than to make it more plaine.

Secondly, whereas some of these rules haue a concurrence with the ciuill Romane law, and some others a diuersity, and many times an opposition,such grounds which are common to our law and theirs I haue not affected to disguise into other words than the Ciuilians vse, to the end they might seem inuented by me,& not borrowed or translated from them: No, but I tooke hold of it as matter of greater Authority and Maiestie to see and consider the concordance be-

tweene

tweene the lawes penn'd, and as it were dicted *verbatim* by the same reason : on the other side, the diuersities betweene the ciuill Romane rules of law and ours, happening either when there is such an indifferency of reason, so equally ballanced as the one law imbraceth one course, and the other the contrary, and both iust after either is once positiue and certaine, or where the lawes varie in regard of accōmodating the law to the different considerations of estate, I haue not omitted to set downe.

Thirdly, whereas I could haue digested these rules into a certaine method or order, which I know would haue beene more admired, as that which would haue made euery particular rule through coherence and relation vnto other rules seeme more cunning and deepe, yet I haue auoided so to doe, because this deliuering of knowledge in distinct and disioyned Aphorismes doth leaue the wit of man more free to turne and tosse, and make vse of that which is so deliuered to more seuerall purposes and applications; for wee see that all the ancient wisdome and science was wont to bee deliuered in that forme, as may bee seene by the parables of *Solomon*, and by the Aphorismes of *Hippocrates*, and the morall verses of *Theognes* and *Phocilides*, but chiefely the president of the Ciuill law, which hath taken the same course with their rules, did confirme mee in my opinion.

 Fourthly,

Fourthly, whereas I know verie well it would haue beene more plausible and more currant, if the rules, with the expositions of them had beene set downe either in Latine or in English, that the harshnesse of the language might not haue disgraced the matter, and that Ciuilians, States-men, Schollers, and other sensible men might not haue beene barred from them; yet I haue forsaken that grace and ornament of them, and onely taken this course: The rules themselues I haue put in Latine, not purified further than the propertie of the termes of the law would permit; which language I chose as the briefest to contriue the rules compendiously, the aptest for memory, and of the greatest Authoritie and Maiesty to bee auouched and alledged in argument: and for the expositions and distinctions, I haue retained the peculiar language of our law, because it should not bee singular among the bookes of the same science, and because it is most familiar to the Students and professors thereof, and because that it is most significant to expresse conceits of law; and to conclude, it is a language wherein a man shall not bee inticed to hunt after words, but matter; and for the excluding of any other than professed Lawyers, it was better manners to exclude them by the strangenesse of the language, than by the obscuritie of the conceit, which is, as though it had beene written in no priuate and retired language, yet by those that are not Lawyers would for the

most

most part not haue beene vnderstood, or which is worse, mistaken.

Fiftly, whereas it might haue beene more flourish and ostentation of reading, to haue vouched the authorities, and sometimes to haue enforced or noted vpon them, yet I haue abstained from that also; and the reason is, because I iudged it a matter vndue and preposterous to prooue rules and maximes; wherein I had the example of Mr *Littleton* and Mr *Fitzherbert,* whose writings are the institutions of the lawes of England, whereof the one forbeareth to vouch any authoritie altogether, the other neuer reciteth a booke, but when hee thinketh the case so weake of credit in it selfe, as it needs a surety; and these two I did far more esteeme than Mr *Perckings* or Mr *Stamford* that haue done the contrary: well will it appeare to those that are learned in the lawes, that many of the cases are iudged cases, either within the books or of fresh report, and most of them fortified by iudged cases, and similitude of reason, though in some few cases I did intend expressely to weigh downe the authority by euidence of reason, and therein rather to correct the law than either to sooth a receiued error, or by vnprofitable subtilty, which corrupteth the sense of law, to reconcile contrarieties; for these reasons I resolued not to derogate from the authority of the rules, by vouching of any of the authority of the cases, though in mine owne copy I had them quoted:

for

for although the meannesse of mine owne person may now at first extenuate the authority of this collection, and that euery man is aduentrous to controule, yet surely according to *Gamduells* reason, if it bee of weight, time will settle and authorize it; if it bee light and weake, time will reprooue it: So that, to conclude, you haue here a worke without any glory of affected noueltie, or of method, or of language, or of quotations and authorities, dedicated onely to vse, and submitted onely to the censure of the learned, and chiefly of time.

Lastly, there is one point aboue all the rest, I accompt the most materiall for making these reasons indeed profitable and instructing, which is, that they bee not set downe alone like short darke Oracles which euery man will bee content still to allow to bee true, but in the meane time they giue little light or direction; but I haue attended them, a matter not practised, no not in the Ciuill law to any purpose; and for want whereof, indeed the rules are but as prouerbs and many times plaine fallacies; with a cleere and perspicuous exposition, breaking them into cases, and opening them with distinctions, and sometimes shewing the reasons aboue whereupon they depend, and the affinity they haue with other rules: and though I haue thus with as good discretion and fore-sight as I could, ordered this worke, and as I might say without all colours or showes

husbanded

husbanded it beſt to profit, yet neuertheleſſe not wholly truſting to mine owne iudgement, hauing collected 300. of them, I thought good before I brought them all into forme to publiſh ſome few, that by the taſte of other mens opinions in this firſt, I might receiue either approbation in mine owne courſe, or better aduice for the altering of the other which remaine; for it is great reaſon that that which is intended to the profite of others, ſhould be guided by the conceits of others.

In

REGVLAE.

falsam

HE

THE MAXIMES OF THE LAW.

In jure non remota causa, sed proxima spectatur. Regula I.

T were infinite for the law to judge the causes of causes, and their impulsions one of another, therefore it contenteth it selfe with the immediate cause, and judgeth of acts by that, without looking to any further degree.

As if an annuity be granted *pro consilio impenso & impendendo,* and the grantee commit treason, whereby he is imprisoned, so that the grantor cannot haue accesse vnto him for his counsell, yet neverthelesse the annuity is not determined by this 6. H. 8. Dy.

non feasance; yet it was the grantees act and default to commit the treason, whereby the imprisonment grew: But the law looketh not so farre, but excuseth him, because the not giving counsell was compulsary, and not voluntary, in regard of the imprisonment.

Litt. cap. 2.H.4.3. 26.H.8.2.

So if a Parson make a lease, and be deprived or resigne, the successors shall avoid the lease, and yet the cause of deprivation, and more strongly of a resignation, moved from the partie himselfe; but the law regardeth not that, because the admission of the new incombent is the act of the ordinary.

So if I be seised of an advouson in gross, and an vsurpation bee had against mee, and at the next avoidance I vsurpe arere, I shall be remitted, and yet the presentation, which is the act remoate, is mine owne act: but the admission of my Clerke, whereby the inheritance is reduced to mee, is the act of the Ordinary.

[illegible]H.7.2[illegible]

So if I covenant with I. S. a stranger in consideration of naturall love to my sonne, to stand seised to the vse of the said I. S. to the intent he shall enfeoffe my sonne; by this no vse ariseth to I. S. because the law doth respect that there is no immediate consideration betweene mee and I. S.

So if I be bound to enter into a statute before the Mayor of the Staple at such a day for the securitie

ritie of 100[l]. and the obligee before the day accept of mee a leaſe of an houſe in ſatisfaction, this is no plea in debt vpon my obligation, and yet the end of that ſtatute was but ſecuritie of money: but becauſe the entring into this ſtatute it ſelfe, which is the immediate act whereunto I am bound, is a corporall act which lieth not in ſatisfaction, therefore the law taketh no conſideration that the remoate intent was for money.

So if I make a feoffement in fee, vpon condition that the feoffee ſhall enfeoffe over, and the feoffee be diſſeiſed, and a diſcent caſt, and then the feoffee binde himſelfe in a ſtatute, which ſtatute is diſcharged before the recoverie of the land, this is no breach of the condition, because the land was never liable to the ſtatute, and the poſſibilitie that it ſhould be liable vpon the recoverie, the law doth not reſpect.

M.40.& 41.El. Iulius Winningtons caſe, ore report per le treſreuerend Iudge, le Sur. Coke, lib, 2.

So if I enfeoffe two, vpon condition to enfeoffe, and one of them take a wife, the condition is not broken, and yet there is a remoate poſſibilitie that the iointenant may die, and then the feme is intitled to dower.

So if a man purchaſe land in fee-ſimple, and die without iſſue, in the firſt degree the law reſpecteth dignitie of ſexe and not proximity, and therefore the remote heire on the part of the father ſhall have it before the neere heire on the part

 of

of the mother; but in any degree paramount the first the law respecteth not, and therfore the neere heire by the grand-mother on the part of the father shall have it before the remote heire of the grandfather on the part of the father.

This rule faileth in covenous acts, which though they bee conveighed through many degrees and reaches, yet the law taketh heed to the corrupt beginning, and counteth all as one intire act:

As if a feoffement bee made of lands held by Knights seruice to I. S. vpon condition that within a certaine time hee shall enfeoffe I. D. which feoffement to I. D. shall bee to the vse of the wife of the first feoffor for her iointure, &c. this feoffement is within the statute of 32. *H.* 8. *nam dolus circuitu non purgatur.*

In like manner, this rule holdeth not in criminall acts, except they have a full interruption, because when the intention is matter of substance, and that which the law doth principally behold, there the first motive will bee principally regarded, and not the last impulsion. As if I. S. of malice prepensed discharge a Pistoll at I. D. and misseth him, whereupon hee throwes downe his Pistoll, and flyes, and I. D, pursueth him to kill him, whereupon hee turneth and killeth I. D. with a Dagger; if the law should consider the last impulsive cause, it should say, that it was in his owne defence;

fence; but the law is otherwise, for it is but a pursuance & execution of the first murtherous intent.

But if I. S. had fallen down his Dagger drawne, and I. D. had fallen by haste vpon his Dagger, there I. D. had beene *felo de se*, and I. S. shall goe quit. 44. Ed. 3.

Also you may not confound the act, with the execution of the act; nor the entire act, with the last part or the consummation of the act.

For if a disseisor enter into religion, the immediate cause is from the party, though the discent bee cast in law; but the law doth but execute the act which the party procureth, and therefore the discent shall not binde, *et sic è converso*. Lit. cap. de disc.

If a lease for yeares bee made rendring a rent, and the lessee make a feoffement of part, and the lessor enter, the immediate cause is from the law in respect of the forfeiture, though the entrie bee the act of the party; but that is but the pursuance and putting in execution of the title which the law giveth, and therefore the rent or condition shall bee apportioned. 21. Eliz. 24. H. 8. fo. 4. Dy.

So in the binding of a right by a discent, you are to consider the whole time from the disseisin to the discent cast, and if at all times the person bee not priviledged, the discent bindes.

 And

And therefore if a feme covert bee diſſeiſed, and the Baron dieth and ſhee taketh a new huſband, and then the diſcent is caſt: or if a man that is not *infra* 4. *Maria*, bee diſſeiſed, and hee returne into England, and goe over ſea againe, and then a diſcent is caſt, this diſcent bindeth becauſe of the *interim* when the perſons might have entered, and the law reſpecteth not the ſtate of the perſon at the laſt time of the diſcent caſt, but a continuance from the verie diſſeiſed to the diſcent.

9.H.7.24.

3.& 4.P.& M. Br 143.

So if Baron and feme bee, and they ioine in a feoffement of the wives land rendring a rent, and the Baron dye, and the feme take a new husband before any rent day and hee accepteth the rent, the feoffement is affirmed for ever.

Regula 2.

Non poteſt adduci exceptio ejuſdem rei, cujus petitur diſſolutio.

IT were impertinent and contrary in it ſelfe, for the law to allow of a plea in barre of ſuch matter as is to bee defeated by the ſame ſuite; for it is included, otherwiſe a man ſhould never come to the end and effect of his ſuite, but bee cut off in the way.

And therefore if tenant intaile of a mannour, whereunto a villeine is regardant, diſcontinue and dye, and the right of the entaile diſcend to the villaine leine himselfe, who brings a *formedon*, and the discontinuee pleadeth villenage, this is no plea, because the devesting of the mannor, which is the intention of the suite, doth include this plea, because it determineth the villenage.

So if tenant in ancient demesne be disseised by the Lord, whereby the seigniory is suspended, and the disseisee bring his assize in the Court of the Lord, Francke fee is no plea, because the suite is brought to vndoe the disseis. and so to revive the seigniory in ancient demesne.

So if a man be attainted and executed, and the 7.H.4.39.
heire bring a writ of error vpon the attaindor, and 7.H.6.44.
the corruption of bloud by the same attaindor bee pleaded to interrupt his conveighing in the same writ of error, this is no plea, for then hee were without remedy ever to reverse the attaindor.

So if tenant intaile discontinue for life rendring a rent, and the issue brings a *formedon*, and the warranty of his ancestor with assets be pleaded against
him, and the assets is laid to bee no other but his 38.Ed.3.32.
reversion with the rent, this is no plea, because the *formedon* which is brought to vndoe this discontinuance doth inclusively vndoe this new reversion in fee with the rent thereunto annexed.

But whether this rule may take place where the matter of plea is not to be avoided in the same suite but in an other suite, is doubtfull; and I rather take the

the law to be that this rule doth extend to ſuch caſes, for otherwiſe the partie were at a miſchiefe, in reſpect the exceptions and barres might bee pleaded croſſe either of them in the contrary ſuite, and ſo the party altogether prevented and intercepted to come by his right.

So if a man bee attainted by two ſeverall attaindors, and there is error in them both, there is no reaſon but that there ſhould be a remedie open for the heire to reverſe thoſe attaindors being erroneous, as well if they bee twentie as one.

And therefore if in a writ of error brought by the heire of one of them, the attaindor ſhould be a plea peremptorily, & ſo againe if in error brought of that other, the former ſhould be a plea, theſe were to exclude him vtterly of his right; and therefore it ſhould be a good replication to ſay that hee hath a writ of error depending of that alſo, and ſo the Court ſhall proceed; but no judgement ſhall be given till both pleas bee diſcuſſed: and if either plea bee found without error, there ſhall bee no reverſall either of the one or of the other: and if hee diſcontinue either writ, then ſhall it bee no longer a plea: and ſo of ſeverall outlawries in a perſonall action.

And this ſeemeth to mee more reaſonable, than that generally an outlawrie or an attaindor ſhould bee no plea in a writ of error brought vpon a diverſe

verſe outlawrie or an attaindor, as 7. *H*. 4. and 7. *H*. 6. ſeeme to hold, for that is a remedy too large for the miſchiefe; for there is no reaſon but if any of the outlawries or attaindors bee indeed without error but it ſhould be a peremptory plea to the perſon in a writ of error as well as in any other action.

But if a man levy a fine Sr *conuſaunce de droit come ceo que il ad de ſon done*, & ſuffer a recoverie of the ſame lands, and there bee error in them both, hee cannot bring error firſt of the fine becauſe by the recovery his title of error is diſcharged and releaſed in law *incluſiuè*, but hee muſt begin with the error vpon the recoverie (which he may do becauſe a fine executed barreth no titles that accrew *de priſne temps* after the fine levied) and ſo reſtore himſelfe to his title of error vpon the fine: but ſo it is not in the former caſe of the attaindor; for a writ of error to a former attaindor is not given away by a ſecond, except it bee by expreſſe words of an act of Parliament, but onely it remaineth a plea to his perſon while hee liveth, and to the conveyance of his heire after his death.

But if a man levy a fine where he hath nothing in the land, which inureth by way of concluſion onely, and is executorie againſt all purchaſes and new titles which ſhall grow to the Conuſor afterwards, and hee purchaſe the land, and ſuffer a recoverie to the Conuſee, and in both fine and recoverie, there is error: This fine is *Ianus Bifrons*, and will looke forward, and barre him of his writ of error brought of the recouery, and therefore it will come to the reason of the first case of the attaindor that hee must reply that hee hath a writ also depending of the same fine, and so demand iudgement.

To returne to our first purpose, like law is it if tenant intaile of two acres make two seuerall discontinuances to seuerall persons for life rendring a rent, and bringeth a *formedon* of both, and in the *formedon* brought of white acre the reuersion and rent reserued vpon blacke acre is pleaded, and so contrary. I take it to bee a good replication that he hath a *formedon* also vpon that depending whereunto the tenant hath pleaded the discent of the reuersion of white acre, and so neither shall bee a barre; and yet there is no doubt but if in a *formedon* the warranty of tenant intaile with assets bee pleaded, it is no replication for the issue to say that a *Precipe* dependeth brought by I. S. to euict the assets.

But the former case standeth vpon the particular reason before mentioned.

Verba

Verba fortius accipiuntur contra proferentem. Reg. 3.

THis rule that a mans deedes and his words shall be taken strongliest against himselfe, though it bee one of the most common grounds of the law, it is notwithstanding a rule drawn out of the depth of reason; for first it is a Schoole-Master of wisdome & diligence in making men watchfull in their owne businesse, next it is author of much quiet and certainty, and that in two sorts; first, because it fauoureth acts and conueyances executed, taking them still beneficially for the grantees and possessors; and secondly, because it makes an end of many questions and doubts about construction of words: for if the labour were onely to picke out the intention of the parties, euery Iudge would haue a seuerall sense, whereas this rule doth giue them a sway to take the law more certainely one way.

But this rule, as all other which are verie generall, is but a sound in the ayre, and commeth in sometimes to helpe and make vp other reasons without any great instruction or direction, except it be duely conceiued in point of difference, where it taketh place, and where not; and first we will examine it in grants, & then in pleadings.

The force of this rule is in three things, in ambiguity of words, in implication of matter, and deducing or qualifying the exposition of such grants as were against the law, if they were taken according to their words.

2. R. 3. 18. 21. H. 7. 29. And therefore if I. S. submit himselfe to arbitrament of all actions and suites betweene him and I. D. and I. N. it rests ambiguous whether the submission shall bee intended collectiue of ioint actions onely, or distributiue of seuerall actions also; but because the words shall be taken strongliest against I. S. that speakes them, it shall bee understood of both: for if I. S. had submitted himselfe to arbitrament of all actions and suites which hee hath now depending, except it bee such as are betweene him and I. D. and I. N. now it shall bee understood collectiue onely of ioint actions, because in the other case large construction was hardest against him that speakes, and in this case strict construction is hardest.

8. Ass. p. 10. So if I graunt ten pounds rent to Baron and feme, and if the Baron dye that the feme shall haue three pounds rent, because these words rest ambiguous whether I intend three pounds by way of encrease or three pounds by way of restraint and abatement of the former rent of ten pounds, it shall bee taken strongliest against mee that am the grauntor, that it is 3 l. addition to the ten; but if I had let land to Baron and feme for three liues, reseruing 10 l. *per annum*, and if the

Baron

Baron dye reſeruing three pounds, this ſhall bee taken contrary to the former caſe, to abbridge my rent onely to three pounds.

So if I demiſe *omnes boſcos meos in villa de dale* for years,this paſſeth the ſoil,but if I demiſe all my lands in dale *exceptis boſcis*,this extendeth to the trees onely and not to the ſoile. 14.H.8. 28.H.8.D. 19.

So if I ſowe my lands with corne, and let it for yeares,the corne paſſeth to my leſſee, if I except it not; but if I make a leaſe for life to I. S. vpon condition that vpon requeſt hee ſhall make mee a leaſe for yeares, and I. S. ſoweth the ground, and then I make requeſt, I. S. may well make me a leaſe excepting his corne, and not breake the condition.

So if I haue free warren in mine owne hand, and let my land for life not mentioning the warren, yet the leaſee by implication ſhall haue the warren diſcharged and extract during his leaſe: but if I let the land *vna cum libera warrenna*, excepting white acre,there the warren is not by implication reſerued vnto mee either to bee inioyed or extinguiſhed, but the leaſee ſhall haue warren againſt mee in white acre. 8.H.7. 32.H.6.

So if I. S. hold of mee by fealty and rent only,and I graunt the rent,not ſpeaking of the fealty, yet the fealty by implication ſhall paſſe,be- 29.Aſſ.pl.10.

 cauſe

cause my grant shall be taken strongly as of a rent seruice and not of a rent secke.

44. Ed. 3. 19. Otherwise had it been if the seigniory had bin by homage fealty and rent, because of the dignity of the seruice which could not haue passed by intendment by the graunt of the rent, but if I be

26. ass. pl. 66. seised of the mannor of dale in fee whereof I. S. holds by fealty and rent, and I graunt the mannor excepting the rent, the fealtie shall passe to the grauntee, and I. S. shall haue but a rent secke.

So in graunts against the law, if I giue land to I. S. and his heires males, this is a good fee-simple; which is a larger estate than the words seeme to intend and the word (males) is voide: But if I make a gift entaile reseruing a rent to me and the heires of my body, the words *(of my body)* are not voide, and to leaue it a rent in fee-simple, but the words (heires) and all are voide, and leaues it but a rent for life, except that you will say it is but a limitation to any my heire in fee-simple which shall bee heire of my body, for it cannot bee a rent entaile by reseruation.

But if I giue land with my daughter in francke marriage, the remaindor to I. S. and his heires, this graunt cannot bee good in all the parts, according to the words, for it is incident to the nature of a gift in francke marriage that the donee hold it of the donor, and therefore my deed shall bee

bee taken so strongly against my selfe* that rather than the remainder shall be voide the franck marriage though it bee first placed in the deede shall bee voide as a francke marriage.

* Quære car le ley séble dẽe le contrary, entant que in vn grant quant lun part del fait ne poit estoier oue lauter le darr: serra void, auterment in vn deuise et accordant fuit lopin: de Sur Anderson et Owen Iust: contra Walmesley Iust: P. 40. Eliz. in le case de Coũtesse de Warwicke et Sur Barkley in com. banco.

But if I giue land in francke marriage reseruing to mee and my heires ten pounds rent, now the franke marriage stands good and the reseruation is voide, because it is a limitation of a benefit to my selfe and not to a stranger.

So if I let white acre, blacke acre, and greene acre to I. S. excepting white acre, his exception is voide, because it is repugnant, but if I let the three acres, aforesaid, rendring twenty shillings rent, *viz.* for white acre ten shillings, and for black acre ten shillings, I shall not destraine at all in greene acre, but that shall bee discharged of my rent. 4. H. 6. 22. 26. als. pl. 66.

So if I grant a rent to I. S. and his heires out of my mannour of *dale & obligo manerium & omnia bona & catella mea super manerium prædictum existentia ad distringendum per Baliuum Domini Regis*: this limitation of the distresse to the Kings Baliffe is voide, and it is good to giue a power of distresse to I. S. the grauntee and his Baliffes. 46. Ed. 3. 18.

But if I giue land intaile *tenend' de capitalibus Dominis per reditum viginti solidorum & fidelitatem*: this limitation of tenure to the Lord is voide, 2. Ed. 4. 5.

Voide, and it shall not be good, as in the other case, to make a reservation of twenty shillings good vnto my selfe, but it shall bee utterly voide as if no reservation at all had beene made; and if the truth bee that I that am the donor hold of the Lord paramount by ten shillings onely, then there shall bee ten shillings onely reserved upon the gift entaile as for ovelty.

21. Ed. 3. 49. 31. & 32. H. 8. Dyer 46. Plow. fo. 37. 15. H. 6. 34.

So if I give land to I. S. and the heires of his body, and for default of such issue *quod tenementum & prædictum revertatur ad I. N.* yet these words of reservation will carry a remainder to a stranger. But if I let white acre to I. S. excepting ten shillings rent, these words of exception to mine owne benefit shall neuer inure to words of reseruation.

But now it is to bee noted, that this rule is the last to bee resorted to, and is neuer to bee relied vpon but where all other rules of exposition of words faile; and if any other come in place, this giueth place. And that is a point worthy to bee obserued generally in the rules of the law, that when they encounter and crosse one anothe in any case, it bee vnderstood which the law holdeth worthier, and to bee preferred; and it is in this particular very notable to consider, that this being a rule of some strictnesse and rigour, doth not as it were it's office, but in absence of other rules which are of more equity and humanity; which

which rules you shall afterwards finde set downe with their expositions and limitations.

But now to giue a taste of them to this present purpose, it is a rule that generall words shall neuer bee stretched too farre in intendment, which the Ciuilians vtter thus. *Verba generalia restringuntur ad habilitatem personæ, vel ad aptitudinem rei.*

Therefore if a man grant to another Common *intra metas & bundas villæ de dale*, and part of the ville is his seuerall, and part his waste and Common; the grantee shall not haue Common in the Seuerall, and yet that is the strongest exposition against the grantor. 14. Ass. pl. 21.

So it is a rule, *verba ita sunt intelligenda, vt res magis valeat quam pereat*: and therefore if I giue land to I. S. and his heires *reddend' quinque libras annatim* to I. D. and his heires, this implies a condition to mee that am the grantor; yet it were a stronger exposition against mee, to say the limitation should bee voide, and the feoffement absolute. Lit. cap. Cond.

So it is a rule, that the law will not intend a wrong, which the Ciuilians vtter thus: *Ea est accipienda interpretatio, quæ vitio caret.* And therefore if the executor of I. S. grant *omnia bona & catella sua*, the goods which they haue as execu- 10. Ed. 4. 1.

tors

tors will not passe, because *non constat* whether it may bee a deuastation, and so a wrong; and yet against the trespasser that taketh them out of their hand, they shall declare *quod bona sua cepit.*

So it is a rule, that words are so to bee vnderstood, that they worke somewhat, and bee not idle and friuolous: *verba aliquid operari debent, verba cum effectu sunt accipienda.* And therefore if I buy and sell you the fourth part of my mannor of dale, and say not in how many parts to be diuided, this shall bee construed foure parts of fiue, and not of 6. nor 7. &c. because that it is the strongest against mee; but on the other side, it shall not bee intended foure parts of foure parts, or the whole or foure quarters; and yet that were strongest of all, but then the words were idle and of none effect.

3.H.6.20. So it is a rule, *Deuinatio non interpretatio est, quæ omnino recedit à litera:* and therefore if I haue a fee farme rent issuing out of white acre of ten shillings, and I reciting the same reseruation doe grant to I. S. the rent of fiue shillings *percipiend' de reddit' predict' & de omnibus terris & tenementis meis in dale* with a clause of distresse, although there bee atturnement yet nothing passeth out of my former rent, and yet that were strongest against mee to haue it a double rent or grant of part of that rent with an enlargement of a distresse in the other land, but for that it is against

gainst the words, because *copulatio verborum indicat acceptionem in eodem sensu*, and the word *de* (*anglice* out of) may be taken in two senses, that is, either as a greater summe out of a lesse, or as a charge out of land or other principall interest; and that the coupling of it with lands & tenemẽts *viz*. I reciting that I am seised of such a rent of ten shillings, doe grant fiue shillings *percipiend' de eodem reddit'* it is good enough without atturnment, because *percipiend de &c.* may well be taken for *parcella de &c.* without violence to the words, but if it had beene *de reddit' predict'* although I. S. bee the person that payeth mee the foresaid rent of ten shillings, yet it is voide, and so it is of all other rules of exposition of grants when they meet in opposition with this rule they are preferred.

Now to examine this rule in pleadings as wee haue done in grants, you shall finde that in all imperfections of pleadings whether it bee in ambiguity of words and double intendments, or want of certainty and auerments, the plea shall be strictly and strongly against him that pleads.

For ambiguity of words, if in a writ of entrie vpon disseisin, the tenant pleads iointenancy with I. S. of the gift and feoffement of I. D. iudgemẽt *de briefe* the demandant saith that long time before I. D. any thing had the demandant himselfe was seised in fee *quousque predict. I. D.*

 super

super possessionem eius intrauit, and made a ioint feoffement, whereupon he the demandant reentred and so was seised vntill by the defendant alone hee was disseised; this is no plea, because the word *intrauit* may bee vnderstood either of a lawfull entrie, or of a tortious, and the hardest against him shall bee taken, which is, that it was a lawfull entrie, therefore he should haue alledged precisely that I. D. *disseisiuit*.

3. Ed.6, Dy.66. So vpon ambiguities that grow by reference, If an action of debt bee brought against I. N. and I. P. Sheriffes of London vpon an escape, and the plaintiffe doth declare vpon an execution by force of a recouerie in the prison of Ludgate *sub custodia I. S. & I. D.* then Sheriffes in 1. K. H. 8. and that hee so continued *sub custodia I. B. & I. G.* in 2. King H. 8. and so continued *sub custodia I. N. & I. L.* in 3. K. H. 8. and then was suffered to escape: I. N. & I. L. plead that before the escape supposed at such a day *anno superius in narratione specificato* the said I. D. and I. S. *ad tunc vicecomites* suffered him to escape, this is no good plea, because there bee three yeares specified in the declaration, and it shall be hardest taken that it was 1. or 3. H. 8. when they were out of office. and yet it is neerely induced by the *ad tunc vicecomites* which should leaue the intendment to be of that yeare in which the declaration supposeth that they were Sheriffes, but that sufficeth not, but the yeare must be alledged in

in fact, for it may bee mislaid by the plaintiffe, and therefore the defendants meaning to discharge themselues by a former escape, which was not in their time, must alledge it precisely.

For incertainty of intendment, If a warranty collaterall be pleaded in barre, and the plaintiffe by replication to auoide the warranty, saith, that hee entred vpon the possession of the defendant, *non constat* whether this entrie was in the life of the ancestor or after the warranty attached: and therefore it shall bee taken in hardest sense, that it was after the warranty descended, if it bee not otherwise auerred. 26. H. 8.

For impropriety of words, If a man pleade that his ancestor died by protestation seised, and that I. S. abated &c. this is no plea, for there cannot bee an abatement except there bee a dying seised alledged in fact, and an abatement shal not be improperly taken for disseisin in pleading *car parols sont pleas*.. 38. H. 6. 18. 39. H. 6. 5.

For repugnancie, if a man in auowrie declare that he was seised in his demesne as of fee of white acre, and being so seised did demise the said white acre to I. S. *habendum* the moitie for 21. yeares from the date of the deed, the other moity from the surrender, expiration, or determination of the estate of I. D. *qui tenet prædict' medietatem ad terminum vitæ suæ reddend'* xl. s.

 rent,

rent, this declaration is insufficient, because the seisin that he hath alledged in himselfe in his demesne as of fee in the whole, and the state for life of a moitie are repugnant, and it shall not bee cured by taking the last which is expressed to controll the former, which is but generall and formall, but the plea is naught, and yet the matter in law had bin good to haue intituled him to haue distrained for the whole rent.

But the same restraint followes this rule in pleading that was before noted in grants: for if the case bee such as falleth within another rule of pleading this rule may not be vrged.

9. Ed. 4. 4. Ed. 6. Plow. And therefore it is a rule that a barre is good to a common intent, though not to euerie intent. As, if a debt be brought against fiue executors, and three of them make default, and two appeare and plead in barre a recouerie had against them two of 300 l. and nothing in their hands ouer and aboue that summe. If this barre should be taken strongliest against them, it should be intended that they might haue abated the first suite, because the other three were not named, and so the recouery not duely had against them; but because of this other rule the barre is good: for that the more common intent will say that they two did onely administer, and so the action well considered, rather than to imagine that they would haue lost the benefit and aduantage of abating the writ.

So

So there is another rule, that in pleading a man ſhall not diſcloſe that which is againſt himſelfe: and therefore if it be matter that is to be ſet forth on the other ſide, then the plea ſhall not be taken in the hardeſt ſenſe but in the moſt beneficall, and to bee left vnto the contrarie partie to alleage.

And therefore if a man bee bound in an obligation that if the feme of the obligee doe decease before the feaſt of Saint Iohn the Baptiſt which ſhall bee in the yeare of our Lord God 1598. without iſſue of her bodie by her husband lawfully begotten then liuing, that then the bond ſhall bee void, and in debt brought vpon this obligation, the defendants plead that the feme died before the ſaid feaſt without iſſue of her bodie then liuing: if this plea ſhould bee taken ſtrongliest againſt the defendant, then ſhould it be taken that the feme had iſſue at the time of her death, but this iſſue died before the feaſt; but that ſhall not bee ſo vnderſtood becauſe it makes againſt the defendant, and it is to bee brought in of the plaintiffes ſide, and that without trauerſe. 28. H. 8. Dy. fol. 17.

So if in a detinue brought by a feme againſt the executors of her husband for her reaſonable part of the goods of her husband, and her demand is of a moitie, and ſhe declares vpon the cuſtome of the Realme by which the feme is to

haue

haue a moitie, if no issue bee had betweene her and her husband, and the third part if there bee issue had, and declareth that her husband dieth without issue had betweene them; if this count should bee hardliest construed against the partie, it should be intended that her husband had issue by another wife, though not by her, in which case the feme is but to haue the third part likewise; but that shall not be so intended because it is matter of reply to be shewed of the other side.

And so it is of all other rules of pleadings, these being sufficient not onely for the exact expounding of these other rules, but *obiter* to shew how this rule which we handle is put by when it meetes with anie other rule.

As for Acts of Paliament, Virdicts, Iudgements, &c. which are not words of parties: in them this rule hath no place at all, neither in deuises and wils vpon seuerall reasons, but more especially it is to bee noted, that in euidence it hath no place, which yet seemes to haue some affinitie with pleadings, specially when demurrer is ioined vpon the euidence.

And therfore if land be giuen by will by H. C. to his sonne I. C. and the heires males of his bodie begotten; the remainder to F. C. and the heires males of his bodie begotten; the remainder to the heires males of the bodie of the deuisor;

for, the remainder to his daughter S.C. and the heires of her bodie, with a clause of perpetuitie, and the question comes vpon the point of forfeiture in an assize taken by default, and euidence is giuen, and demurrer vpon euidence, and in the euidẽce giuen to maintain the entry of the daughter vpon a forfeiture, it is not set forth nor auerred that the deuisor had no other issue male, yet the euidence is good enough, and it shall bee so intended; and the reason hereof cannot bee, because a Iury may take knowledge of matters not within the euidence, and the Court contrariwise cannot take knowledge of any matters not within the pleas: for it is cleere, that if the euidence had been altogether remote, and not prouing the issue, there, although the Iury might find it, yet a demurrer might well bee taken vpon the euidence.

But if I take the reason of difference to be betweene pleadings, which are but openings of the case, and euidences which are the proofes of an issue, for pleadings being but to open the veritie of the matter in fact indifferently on both parts, hath no scope and conclusion to direct the construction and intendment of them, and therefore must be certaine, but in euidence and proofs the issue which is the state of the question and conclusion shall encline and apply all the proofes as tending to that conclusion.

 Another

Another reason is, that pleadings must be certain, because the aduerse party may know whereto to answer, or else he were at a mischief, which mischiefe is remedied by demurrer; but in euidence if it be short, impertinent or incertaine, the aduerse party is at no mischiefe, because it is to be thought that the Iury will passe against him; yet neuerthelesse the Iury is not compellable to supply the defect of euidence out of their owne knowledge, though it bee in their libertie so to doe, therefore the law alloweth a demurrer vpon euidence also.

Regula 4. *Quod sub certa forma concessum vel reseruatum est non trahitur ad valorem vel compensationem.*

THe Law permitteth euery man to part with his owne interest, and to qualifie his owne graunt as it pleaseth himselfe, and therefore doth not admit any allowance or recompence if the thing be not taken as it is graunted.

So in all profites *a prender*, if I graunt Common for ten beasts, or ten loads of wood out of my Copps, or ten loads of hay out of my Meads to be taken for three yeares, hee shall not haue Common for thirty beasts, or thirty loads of wood or hay the third yeare if hee forbeare for the

37.H.6.10.

the ſpace of two yeares, here the time is certain and preciſe.

So if the place be limitted, or if I graunt Eſtouers to bee ſpent in ſuch a houſe, or ſtone towards the reparation of ſuch a Caſtle, although the grauntee doe burne of his fuell and repaire of his owne charge, yet hee can demand no allowance for that he tooke it not.

So if the kinde be ſpecified, as if I let my Park reſeruing to my ſelfe all the Deere and ſufficient paſture for them, if I do decay the game whereby there is no Deere, I ſhall not haue quantitie of paſture anſwerable to the feed of ſo many Deere as were vpon the ground when I let it, but am without any remedy except I repleniſh the ground againe with Deere.

But it may be thought that the reaſon of theſe caſes is the default and lacheſs of the grauntor, which is not ſo.

For put the caſe that the houſe where the Eſtouers ſhould bee ſpent bee ouerthrown by the act of God, as by tempeſt, or burnt by the enemies of the King, yet there is no recompence to be made.

And in the ſtrongeſt caſe where it is in default of the grauntor, yet he ſhall make void his owne graunt rather than the certain forme of it ſhould be wreſted to an equitie or valuation.

As if I graunt Common *vbicunque averia mea ierint*, the Commoner cannot otherwiſe entitle himſelfe, except that hee auerre that in ſuch grounds my beaſts haue gone and fed, and if I neuer put in any but occupie my grounds otherwiſe, hee is without remedy; but if I put in, and after by pouerty or otherwiſe I deſiſt, yet the Commoner may continue; contrariwiſe, if the words of the graunt had beene *quandocunque averia mea ierint*, for there it depends continually vpon the putting in of my beaſts, or at leaſt the generall ſeaſons when I put them in, not vpon euery houre or moment.

But if I graunt *tertiam aduocationem* to I. S. if hee neglect to take his turne *ea vice*, hee is without remedy: But if my wife bee before intituled to dower, and I dye, then my heire ſhall haue two preſentments, and my wife the third, and my grauntee ſhall haue the fourth; and it doth not impugne this rule at all, becauſe the graunt ſhall receiue that conſtruction at the firſt that it was intended, ſuch an auoidance as may be taken and enioied: as if I graunt *proximam aduocationem*
29. H. 8. Dy. 38. to I. D. and then graunt *proximam aduocationem* to I. S. this ſhall be intended the next to the next, which I may lawfully graunt or diſpoſe. *Quare*.

But

But if I graunt *proximam aduocationem* to I. S. and I. N. is Incumbent, and I graunt by precise words *illam aduocationem quam post mortem, resignationem, translationem, vel depriuationem I. N. immediate fore contigerit*, now the grant is meerely voide, because I had graunted that before, and it cannot bee taken against the words.

Necessitas inducit priuilegium quoad iura priuata. Regula 5.

THe law chargeth no man with default where the act is compulsorie, and not voluntary, and where there is not a consent and election; and therefore if either there bee an impossibility for a man to doe otherwise, or so great a perturbation of the iudgement and reason as in presumption of law mans nature cannot ouercome, such necessity carrieth a priuiledge in it selfe. 4. Ed. 6. Cond.

Necessity is of three sorts, necessity of conseruation of life, necessity of obedience, and necessity of the act of God or of a stranger. Stamf.

First of conseruation of life, If a man steale viands to satisfie his present hunger, this is no felony nor larceney. Stamf.

So if diuers bee in danger of drowning by the casting away of some boate or barge, and one of them get to some plancke, or on the boates side to keepe himselfe aboue water, and another to saue his life thrust him from it, whereby hee is drowned; this is neither *se defendendo* nor by misaduenture, but iustifiable.

Cond.13.6.per Brook. 15.H.7.2. per Keble. 14.H.7.29. per Reade.

So if diuers felons bee in a Iaile, and the Iaile by casualty is set on fire, whereby the prisoners get forth, this no escape, nor breaking of prison.

4.Ed.6.pl. 4.Ed.6.20.condic.

So vpon the Statute, that euery Merchant that setteth his merchandize on land without satisfying the Customer or agreeing for it (which agreement is construed to bee incertainty) shall forfeit his merchandize, and it is so that by tempest a great quantity of the merchandize is cast ouer board, whereby the Merchant agrees with the Customer by estimation, which falleth out short of the truth, yet the ouer-quantity is not forfeited; where note that necessity dispenseth with the direct letter of a Statute law.

Lit.pl.4.19. 12.H.4.20. 14 H.4.30. B.38.H.6.11. 28.H.6.8. 39.H.6.50.

So if a man haue right to land, and doe not make his entrie for terror of force, the law allowes him a continuall claime, which shall bee as beneficiall vnto him as any entry; so shall a man saue his default of appearance by *cretein de eau*, and auoide his debt by *duresse*, whereof you shall finde proper cases elsewhere.

The second necessity is of obedience, and therfore

fore where Baron and Feme commit a felony, the Feme can neither be principall nor accessary, because the law intends her to haue no will, in regard of the subiection and obedience shee owes to her husband. Stamf.26.2. Ed.3.160. cor Fitzh.

So one reason amongst others why Embassadors are vsed to bee excused of practices against the State where they reside, except it be in point of conspiracie, which is against the law of Nations, and society, is, because *non constat* whether they haue it *in mandatis*, and then they are excused by necessity of obedience.

So if a warrant or precept come from the King to fell wood vpon the ground whereof I am tenant for life or for yeares, I am excused in wast.

The third necessitie is of the act of God, or of a stranger, as if I bee particular tenant for yeares of a house, and it be ouerthrowne by grand tempest, or thunder and lightning, or by sudden flouds, or by inuasion of enemies; or if I haue belonging vnto it some Cottage which hath beene infected, whereby I can procure none to inhabite them, no workeman to repaire them, and so they fall down, In all these cases I am excused in wast: but of this last learning when and how the act of God and strangers doe excuse, there bee other particular rules. B.42.Ed.3.6. B.Wast.31. 42.Ed.3.6. 19.Ed.3.per Th.Fitzh.Wast 30. 32.Ed.3. Fitzh.Wast. 105. 44.Ed.3.31.

But

But then it is to be noted, that necessitie priuiledgeth onely *quoad iura priuata*, for in all cases if the act that should deliuer a man out of the necessitie be against the Common-wealth, necessity excuseth not: for *priuilegium non valet contra Rempublicam*; and as another saith, *Necessitas publica maior est quam priuata*: for death is the last and farthest point of particular necessitie, and the law imposeth it vpon euerie subiect, that he preferre the vrgent seruice of his Prince and Countrey before the safety of his life; As if in danger of tempest those that are in the ship throw ouer other mens goods, they are not answerable: but if a man bee commanded to bring Ordnance or Munition to relieue any of the Kings towns that are distressed, then hee cannot for any danger of tempest iustifie the throwing of them ouerboard, for there it holdeth which was spoken by the Romane when he alledged the same necessitie of weather to hold him from imbarquing, *Necesse est vt eam non vt viuam*. So in the case put before of husband and wife, if they ioyne in committing treason, the necessity of obedience doth not excuse the offence as it doth in felony, because it is against the Common-wealth.

13. H. 8. 16. per Shelley. 12. H. 8. 10. per Brooke 22. Ass. pl. 56.

So if a fire be taken in a street, I may iustifie the pulling down of the wall or house of another man to saue the row from the spreading of the fire; but if I be assailed in my house in a Citie or Towne;

Towne, and distressed, and to saue my life I set fire on mine owne house, which spreadeth and taketh hold vpon other houses adioyning, this is not iustifiable, but I am subiect to their action vpon the case, because I cannot rescue mine owne life by doing any thing which is against the Common-wealth: But if it had beene but a priuate trespasse, as the going ouer anothers ground, or the breaking of his inclosure when I am pursued for the safegard of my life, it is iustifiable. 6.Ed.4.7. per Saresi.

This rule admitteth an exception when the Law doth intend some fault or wrong in the partie that hath brought himselfe into the necessitie: so that is *necessitas culpabilis*. This I take to bee the chiefe reason, why *seipsum defendendo* is not matter of Iustification, because the law intends it hath a commencement vpon an vnlawfull cause, because quarrels are not presumed to grow without some wrongs either in words or deedes on either part, and the law that thinketh it a thing hardly triable in whose default the quarrell beganne, supposeth the partie that kils another in his owne defence not to bee without malice; and therefore as it doth not touch him in the highest degree, so it putteth him to sue out his pardon of course, and punisheth him by forfeiture of goods: for where there cannot be anie malice nor wrong presumed, as where a man assailes mee to robbe mee, and I kill him that assaileth me; or if a woman kill him that assaileth 4.H.7.2.

her

her to rauish her it is iustificable without anie pardon.

21.H.7.13. So the common case proueth this exception, that is, if a mad man commit a felonie hee shall not lose his life for it, because his infirmity came by the Act of God; but if a drunken man commit a felonie, he shall not be excused because his imperfection came by his owne default; for the reason and losse of depriuation of will and election by necessitie and by infirmitie is all one, for the lacke of (*arbitrium solutum*) is the matter: and therefore as *infirmitas culpabilis* excuseth not, no more doth *necessitas culpabilis*.

Regula 6. *Corporalis iniuria non recipit æstimationem de futuro.*

THe law in many cases that concerne lands or goods doth depriue a man of his present remedie, and turneth him ouer to a further Cirquit of remedie, rather than to suffer an inconuenience: but if it bee question of personall paine, the law will not compell him to sustaine it and expect remedie, because it holdeth no damage a sufficient recompence for a wrong which is corporall.

3.H.4.20. As if the Sheriffe make a false returne that I am

am summoned whereby I lose my land; yet because of the inconuenience of drawing all things to incertaintie and delay, if the Sheriffes returne should not be credited, I am excluded of my auerment against it, and am put to mine action of deceit against the Sheriffe and Summoners; but if the Sheriffe vpon a *Cap.* returne a *Cepi corpus & quod est languidus in prisona*, there I may come in and falsifie the return of the Sheriffe to saue my imprisonment. 3.H.6.35.

So if a man menace me in my goods, and that he will burne certaine euidences of my land which he hath in his hand, if I will not make vnto him a bond, yet if I enter into bond by this terror, I cannot auoid it by plea, because the law holdeth it an incouenience to auoid a speciallitie by such matter of auerrement, and therefore I am put to mine action against such a menacer: but if hee restraine my person, or threaten mee with a battery or with the burning of my house, which is a safetie and protection to my person, or with burning an instrument of manumission, which is an euidence of my enfranchisement; if vpon such menace or duresse I make a deede, I shall auoid it by plea. 7.E.4.20.

So if a trespasser driue away my beasts ouer anothers ground, I pursue them to rescue them, yet am I a trespasser to the stranger vpon whose ground I came; but if a man assaile my person, and 19.H.8.19. 21.H.7.28.

and I fly ouer anothers ground, now am I no trespasser.

This ground some of the Canonists doe aptly inferre out of Christs sacred mouth; *Amen est corpus supra vestimentum*, where they say *vestimentum* comprehendeth all outward things appertaining to a mans condition, as lands and goods, which they say, are not in the same degree with that which is corporall; and this was the reason of the ancient *lex talionis, oculus pro oculo, dens pro dente*, so that by that law *corporalis iniuria de præterito non recepit æstimationem:* But our law when the iniury is already executed and inflicted, thinketh it best satisfaction to the party grieued to relieue him in damage, and to giue him rather profit than reuenge; but it will neuer force a man to tolerate a corporall hurt, and to depend vpon that inferiour kind of satisfaction, *vt in dāmagijs*.

Regula 7.

Excusat aut extenuat delictum in capitalibus, quod non operatur idem in ciuilibus.

IN Capitall causes *in fauorem vitæ*, the law will not punish in so high a degree, except the malice of the will and intention appeare; but in Ciuill trespasses and iniuries that are of an inferiour nature, the law doth rather consider the damage of the party wronged, than the malice of him that was the wrong doer; and therefore,

The

The law makes a difference betweene killing a man vpon malice fore-thought, and vpon present heate: But if I giue a man slanderous words, whereby I damnifie him in his name and credit, it is not materiall whether I vse them vpon suddaine choler and prouocation, or of set malice; but in an action vpon the case, I shall render damages alike.

So if a man bee killed by misaduenture, as by an arrow at Buts, this hath a pardon of course: but if a man bee hurt or maimed onely, an action of trespasse lieth, though it be done against the parties minde and will, and he shall bee punished in the law, as deepely as if hee had done it of malice. Stamf. 16. 6. Ed. 4. 7.

So if a Surgeon authorized to practise, doe through negligence in his cure cause the party to dye, the Surgeon shall not bee brought in question of his life; and yet if hee doe onely hurt the wound whereby the cure is cast backe, and death ensues not, hee is subiect to an action vpon the case for his misfeisance. Stamf. 16.

So if Baron and Feme bee, and they commit felony together, the Feme is neither principall nor accessary, in regard of her obedience to the will of her husband; but if Baron and Feme ioine in committing a trespasse vpon land or otherwise, the action may bee brought against them both.

So if an infant within yeares of discretion, or a mad-man kill another, hee shall not bee impeached thereof; but if they put out a mans eye, or
35.H.6.11. doe him like corporall hurt, hee shall be punished in trespasse.

So in felonies the law admitteth the difference of principall and accessarie, and if the principall dye, or bee pardoned, the proceeding against the accessary faileth; but in a trespasse, if one com-
17.H.4.19. mand his man to beate you, and the seruant after the battery dye, yet your action of trespasse stands good against the Master.

Regula 8. *Æstimatio præteriti delicti ex postremo facto nunquam crescit.*

THe law construeth neither penall lawes, nor penall facts by intendments, but considereth the offence in degree, as it standeth at the time when it is committed; so as if any circumstance or matter bee subsequent, which laide together with the beginning should seeme to draw to it a higher nature, yet the law doth not extend or amplifie the offence.

11.H.4.12. Therefore if a man bee wounded, and the percussor is voluntarily let go at large by the Iailor, and after death ensueth of the hurt, yet this is no felonious escape in the Iailor.

So

So if the Villein ſtrike the heire apparant of the Lord, and the Lord dieth before, and the perſon hurt who ſucceedeth to be Lord to the Villeine dieth after, yet this is no pettie treaſon.

So if a man compaſſe and imagineth the death of one that after commeth to bee King of the Land, not beeing any perſon mentioned within the Statute of 25.Ed.3. this imagination precedent is not high treaſon.

So if a man vſe ſlanderous words of a perſon vpon whom ſome dignitie after deſcends that maketh him a Peere of the Realme, yet he ſhall haue but a ſimple action of the caſe, and not in the nature of a *ſcandalum Magnatum* vpon the ſtatute.

So if Iohn Stile ſteale 6^{d}. from mee in monie, and the King by his proclamation doth raiſe monies, that the weight of ſiluer in the piece now of 6^{d}. ſhould goe for 12^{d}. yet this ſhall remaine pettie larcenie and no felonie; and yet in all ciuill reckonings the alteration ſhall take place: as if I contract with a labourer to doe ſome worke for 12^{d}. and the inhaunſing of monie commeth before I pay him, I ſhall ſatisfie my contract with a ſixepenny piece ſo raiſed.

So if a man deliuer goods to one to keepe, and after retain the ſame perſon into his ſeruice, who

28.H.8.pl.2. who afterwards goeth away with his goods, this is no felony by the statute of 21.H.8. because he was no seruant at that time.

In like manner, if I deliuer goods to the seruant of I. S. to keepe, and after die and make I.S. my executor, and before any new commandement of I. S. to his seruant for the custodie of the same goods, his seruant goeth away with them; this is also out of the same statute. *quod nota.*

But note that it is said *præteriti delicti*; for any accessory before the fact is subiect to all the contingencies pregnant of the fact if they bee pursuances of the same fact: As if a man com-
18.Eliz.175. mand or counsell one to robbe a man, or beate him grieuously and murther ensue, in either case he is accessarie to the murther; *quia in criminalibus præstantur accidentia.*

Regula.9. *Quod remedio destituitur ipsa re valet si culpa absit.*

THe benignitie of the law is such, as when to preserue the principles and grounds of law it depriueth a man of his remedie without his owne fault, it will rather put him in a better degree and condition than in a worse; for if it disable him to pursue his action or to make his claime,

claime, ſometimes it will giue him the thing it ſelfe by operation of law without any act of his owne, ſometimes it will giue him a more beneficiall remedie.

And therefore if the heire of the diſſeiſor which is in by diſcent make a leaſe for life, the remainder for life vnto the diſſeiſee, and the leſſee for life die, now the franketenement is caſt vpon the diſſeiſee by act in law, and thereby hee is diſabled to bring his *Precipe* to recouer his right, whereupon the law iudgeth him in his ancient right as ſtrongly as if it had beene recouered and executed by action, which operation of law is by an ancient terme & word of law called a remitter; but if there may bee aſſigned any default or laches in him, either in accepting the free hold, or in accepting the intereſt that drawes the free hold, then the law denieth him anie ſuch benefit.

And therfore if the heire of the diſſeiſor make a leaſe for yeares the remainder in fee to the diſſeiſee, the diſſeiſee is not remitted, and yet the remainder is in him without his own knowledge or aſſent; but becauſe the free hold is not caſt vpon him by act in law it is no remitter. *quod nota.* Lit.pl.683.

So if the heire of the diſſeiſor infeoffe the diſſeiſee and a ſtranger, and make him liuerie, al- Lit.pl.685.

 though

though the ſtranger die before any agreement or taking of the profits by the diſſeiſee, yet he is not remitted, becauſe though a moitie bee caſt vpon him by ſuruiuor, yet that is but *Ius accreſcendi*, and it is no caſting of the free hold vpon him by act in law, but hee is ſtill as an immediate purchaſor, and therefore no remitter.

Semble in ceſt caſe clerement le ley dée contrarie.

So if the husband bee ſeiſed in the right of his wife, and diſcontinue and dieth, and the feme takes another husband, who takes a feoffement from the diſcontinuee to him and his wife, the feme is not remitted; and the reaſon is, becauſe ſhee was once ſole, and ſo a laches in her for not purſuing her right: but if the feoffement taken backe had been to the firſt husband and her ſelfe, ſhe had been remitted.

Lit.pl.666.

1. M Condic.3.

Yet if the husband diſcontinue the lands of the wife, and the diſcontinuee make a feoffement to the vſe of the husband and wife, ſhee is not remitted; but that is vpon a ſpeciall reaſon, vpon the letter of the ſtatute of 27.H.8. of vſes, that willeth that the *ceſtuy que vſe* ſhall haue the poſſeſſion in qualitie and degree as he had the vſe; but that holdeth place onely vpon the firſt veſting of the vſe; for when the vſe is abſolutely executed and veſted, then it doth inſue meerely the nature of poſſeſſions; as if the diſcontinuee had made a feoffement in fee to the vſe of I. S. for life,

34.H.8.Dyer 3 ℞.

life, the remainder to the vse of baron and feme, and lessee for life die, now the feme is remitted, *causa qua supra.*

Also if the heire of the disseisor make a lease for life, the remainder to the disseisee who chargeth the remainder, and the lessee for life dies, the disseisee is not remitted; and the reason is, his intermeddling with the wrongfull remainder, whereby he hath affirmed the same to be in him, and so accepted it: but if the heire of the disseisor had granted a rent charge to the disseisee, and afterwards made a lease for life, the remainder to the disseisee, and the lessee for life had died, the disseisee had been remitted, because there appeareth no assent or acceptance of anie estate in the free hold, but onely of a collaterall charge.

So if the feme be disseised and intermarry with the disseisor, who makes a lease for life, rendring rent, and dieth leauing a sonne by the same feme, 6.Ed.3.17. and the sonne accepts the rent of the lessee for life, and then the feme dies, and the lessee for life dies, the sonne is not remitted, yet the franketenement was cast vpon him by act in law, but be- 28.H.8.pl.20. cause hee had agreed to be in the tortious reuersion by acceptance of the rent, therefore no remitter.

So if tenant intaile discontinue, and the discontinuee make a lease for life, the remainder to

 the

the Issue intaile beeing within age and at full age, the lessee for life surrendreth to the issue intaile and tenant intaile dies, and lessee for life dies, yet the same issue is not remitted; and yet if the issue had accepted a feoffement within age, and had continued the taking of the profits when hee came of full age, and then the tenant intaile had died, notwithstanding his taking of the profits he had beene remitted: for that which guides the remitter, is, if he be once in of the free hold without any laches: as if the heire of the disseisor enfeoffes the heire of the disseisee who dies, and it descends to a second heire vpon whom the frank tenement is cast by discent, who enters and takes the profits, and then the disseisee dies, this is a remitter, *causa qua supra*.

Lit. pl. 3.6. Also if tenant intaile discontinue for life, and take a surrender of the leasee, now hee is remitted and seised againe by force of the taile, and yet hee commeth in by his owne act: but this case differeth from all other cases, because the discontinuance was but particular at first, and the new gained reuersion is but by intendment and necessity of law; and therefore is but as it were *ab initio*, with a limitation to determine whensoeuer the particular discontinuance endeth, and the state commeth backe to the ancient right.

To proceed from cases of remitter, which is a great branch of this rule, to other cases; If executors

cutors do redeeme goods pledged by their testator with their owne money, the law doth conuert so much goods as doth amount to the value of that they laide forth, to themselues in property, and vpon a plea of fully administred it shall bee allowed: the reason is, because it may bee matter of necessitie, for the well administring of the goods of the testator, and executing their trust that they disburst money of their owne: for else perhaps the goods would bee forfeited, and hee that had them in pledge would not accept other goods but money, and so it is a libertie which the law giues them, and they cannot haue any suite against themselues; and therefore the law giues them leaue to retaine so much goods by way of allowance: and if their bee two executors, and one of them pay the money, hee may likewise retaine against his companion if hee haue notice thereof. 6. H. 8. pl. 3. Dy.

But if there bee an ouerplus of goods, aboue the value of that he shall disburse, then ought he by his claime to determine what goods hee doth elect to haue in value, or else before such election if his companion doe sell all the goods, hee hath no remedy but in Spirituall Court: for to say he should bee tenant in common with himselfe and his companion *pro rata* of that hee doth lay out, the law doth reiect that course for intricatenesse. 3. Eliz. 187. pl. 8.

So if I haue a lease for yeares worth 20l. by

 the

the yeare, and graunt vnto I. D. a rent of 10[l]. a yeare, and after make him my executor, now I. D. shall bee charged with assets ten pounds onely, and the other ten pounds shall be allowed and considered to him; and the reason is, because the not refusing shall bee accounted no laches vnto him, because an executorship is *pium officium*, and matter of conscience and trust, and not like a purchase to a mans owne vse.

19.H.8.pl.7. in fine.
22.Ass.12.F. Rec.in value 23.

Like law it is, where the debtor makes the debtee his executor, the debt shall bee considered in the assets, notwithstanding it bee a thing in action.

2.H.4.21. Cond.185. 2.H.7.5. 37.H 6.32.

So if I haue a rent charge, and graunt that vpon condition, now though the condition be broken, the grantees estate is not defeated till I haue made my claime; but if after such grant my father purchase the land, and it descend to mee, now if the condition be broken, the rent ceaseth without claime: But if I had purchased the land my selfe, then I had extincted mine owne condition, because I had disabled my selfe to make my claime, and yet a condition collaterall is not suspended by taking backe an estate; as if I make a feoffement in fee, vpon condition that I. S. shall marry my daughter, and take a lease for life from my feoffee, if the feoffee breake the condition, I may claime to hold in by my fee-simple; but the case of the charge is otherwise, for if I haue a rent

6.Ed.6.coud. 133.
Lit.pl.13
20.H.7.per Pol.
35.H 6 Fitz. Barr.162.

rent charge issuing out of 20. acres, and graunt the rent ouer vpon condition, and purchase but one acre, the whole condition is extinct, and the possibilitie of the rent by reason of the condition, is as fully destroied as if there had beene no rent in *Esse*.

So if the King graunt to mee the wardship of I. S. the sonne and heire of I. S. when it falleth, because an action of couenant lieth not against the King, I shall haue the thing my selfe in interest. 30.H.6.pl. Graunts 91.

But if I let land to I. S. rendring a rent, with a condition of reentry, and I. S. bee attainted, whereby the lease comes to the King, now the demand vpon this land is gone, which should giue mee benefit of reentrie, and yet I shall not haue it reduced without demaund; and the reason of difference is, because my condition in this case is not taken away in right, but onely suspended by the priuiledge of the possession: for if the King grant the lease ouer, the condition is reuiued as it was. 7.H.6.40.

Also if my tenant for life graunt his estate to the King, now if I will graunt my reuersion ouer, the King is not compellable to atturne, therefore it shall passe by graunt by deede without atturnment.

So

9.Ed.2.Fitz. Attturnments 18.

So if my tenant for life bee, and I graunt my reuersion *per auter vie*, and the grantee dye, liuing *cei que vie*, now the priuity betweene tenant for life and mee is not restored, and I haue no tenant in *esse* to atturne, therefore I may passe my reuersion without atturnement. *quod nota*.

So if I haue a nomination to a Church, and another hath the presentation, and the presentation comes to the King, now because the King cannot bee attendant, my nomination is turned to an absolute patronage.

6.Ed.6.Dy.72.

Vide contra 2. E.3. fo.8. que per presentmét del feme l'aduowson est deueign disimpropriate a touts iours quel est agree in Sir Cok.Rep.7.fo. 8.a.

So if a man bee seised of an aduouson, and take a wife, and after title of dower giuen her, ioine in impropriating the Church, and dieth, now because the Feme cannot haue the turne because of the perpetuall incumbency, shee shall haue all the turnes during her life; for it shall not bee disimpropriated to the benefit of the heire contrary to the graunt of tenant in fee-simple.

But if a man graunt the third presentment to I.S. and his heires, and impropriate the aduouson, now the grauntee is without remedy, for hee tooke his graunt subiect to that mischiefe at first, and therefore it was his laches, and therefore not like the case of the dower; and this graunt of the third auoidance is not like *tertia pars aduocationis*, or *medietas aduocationis* vpon a tenancy in common of the aduouson; for if two tenants in

common

common bee, and an vsurpation be had against them, and the vsurper doe impropriate, and one of the tenants in common do release, and the other bring his writ of right *de medietate aduocationis* and recouer, now I take the law to bee that because tenants in common ought to ioine in presentment which cannot now be, he shall haue the whole patronage: for neither can there bee an apportionment, that he should present all the turnes, and his incumbent but to haue a moitie of the profits, nor yet the act of impropriation shall not bee defeated. But as if two tenants in common be of a Ward, and they ioine in a writ of right of Ward and one release, the other shall recouer the entire Ward, because it cannot be diuided: so shall it bee in the other case, though it be an inheritance, and though he bring his action alone.

45.Ed.3.

As if a disseisor be disseised, and the first disseisee release to the second disseisor vpon condition, and a descent be cast, and the condition broken; now the meane disseisor whose right is reuiued shal enter notwithstanding this descent, because his right was taken away by the act of a stranger.

Le contrary fuit resolve in Martin Trotts case, pa. 32. Eliz in Com. banco, & Pa. 1. Iac. ib, vide 7. R. 2. Scire fac. 3. 41. E. 3. 14. per Finchden.

But if I deuise land by the statute of 32. H. 8. and the heire of the deuisor enters and makes a feoffement in fee, and the feoffee dieth seised, this descent bindeth, and there shall not bee a

 perpetuall

perpetual liberty of entry vpon the reason that he neuer had seison whereupon he might ground his action, but hee is at a mischiefe by his owne laches: and like law is of the Kings Pattentee; for I see no reasonable difference betweene them and him in the remainder, which is *Littletons* case.

But note, that the Law by operation and matter in fact will neuer counteruaile and supply a title grounded vpon a matter of record, and therfore if I be entituled vnto a writ of error, and the land descend vnto mee, I shall neuer be remitted, no more shall I bee vnto an attaint, except I may also haue a writ of right. 25.H.8.Dy.1.7.

So if vpon my auowry for seruices, my tenant disclaime where I may haue a Writ of right as vpon disclaimer, if the land after descend to me, I I shall neuer be remitted.

Regula 10. *Verba generalia restringuntur ad habilitatem rei vel personæ.*

IT is a rule that the Kings graunts shall not bee taken or construed to a speciall intent; it is not so with the graunts of a common person, for they shall be extended as well to a forrein intent as to a common intent; yet with this exception, that they shall neuer bee taken to an impertinent

or

or a repugnant intent: for all words, whether they bee in deedes or ſtatutes, or otherwiſe if they be general and not expreſſe and preciſe, ſhall bee reſtrained vnto the fitneſſe of the matter or perſon.

As if I graunt common *in omnibus terris meis* in D. and I haue in D. both open grounds and ſeuerall, it ſhall not bee ſtretched to my common in ſeuerall, much leſſe in my Gardens and Orchards. Perk.pl.108.

So if I graunt to a man *omnes arbores meas creſcentes ſuper terras meas in* D. hee ſhall not haue Apple trees or other fruit trees growing in my Gardens or Orchards if there bee any other trees vpon my ground. 14.H.8.2.

So if I graunt to I.S. an annuitie of x.l. a yeare *pro conſilio impenſo & impendendo,* if I. S. bee a Phyſitian, it ſhall bee vnderſtood of his counſell in Phyſicke; and if he bee a Lawyer, of his counſell in Law. 41.Ed.3.6.19.

So if I doe let a tenement to I. S. neere by my dwelling houſe in a Burrough, prouided that hee ſhall not erect or vſe any ſhop in the ſame without my licence, and afterwards I licence him to erect a ſhop, and I.S. is then a Miller, hee ſhall not by vertue of theſe generall words erect a Ioiners ſhop.

16.Eliz.337. Dyer. So the statute of Chantries that willeth all lands to be forfeited, giuen or imploied to a superstitious vse shall not bee construed of the glebe lands of Parsonages: nay further, if the lands be giuen to the Parson of D. to say a Masse in his Church of D. this is out of the statute, because it shall bee intended but as an augmentation of his glebe; but otherwise had it beene if it had beene to say a Masse in any other Church but his owne.

So in the statute of wreckes, that willeth that goods wrackt where any liue domesticall creature remaines in a vessell shall be preserued to the vse of the owner that shallmake his claime by the space of one yeare doth not extend to fresh victuals or the like which is impossible to keepe without perishing or destroying it; for in these and the like cases generall words may bee taken, as was said to a rare and forreine intent, but neuer to an vnreasonable intent.

Regula 11.

Iura sanguinis nullo iure ciuili dirimi possunt.

They bee the very words of the Ciuill law, which cannot bee amended to explaine this rule. *Hæres est nomen Iuris, filius est nomen Naturæ:* therefore corruption of bloud taketh away the priuitie of the one, that is, of the heire, but not of of the other, that is, of the sonne; therefore if a man bee attainted and murthered by a stranger the eldest sonne shall not haue the appeale, because the appeale is giuen to the heire, for the 36.H.6.57.58. youngest sonnes who are equal in bloud shall not 21.Ed.3.17. haue it; but if an attainted person bee killed by his sonne, this is pettie treason, for that the priuitie of a sonne remaineth: for I admit the law to be, that if the sonne kill his father or mother it is pettie treason, and that there remaineth so much in our lawes of the ancient foote-steps of *Potestas patriæ* and naturall obedience, which by the law of God is the very instance it selfe, and all other gouerment and obedience is taken but by equitie, which I had, because some haue thought to weaken the law in that point.

So if land descend to the eldest sonne of a person attainted from his ancestour, of the mother held in Knights seruice, the guardian shall enter, and ouste the father, because the law giueth the father that prerogatiue in respect hee is his sonne and heire; for of a daughter or a speciall heire F.N.Br.fo.143. intaile hee shall not haue it: but if the sonne be attainted, and the father couenant in consideration of naturall loue to stand seised of land to his vse, this is good enough to raise an vse, because the priuity of a naturall affection remaineth.

So if a man be attainted and haue a Charter of pardon, and bee returned of a Iury betweene his ſonne and I. S. the challenge remaineth; for hee may maintaine any ſuite of his ſonne, notwithſtanding the bloud be corrupted.

So by the ſtatute of 21. the Ordinary ought to commit the adminiſtration of his goods that was attainted, and purchaſe his Charter of pardon to his children, though borne before the pardon, for it is no queſtion of inheritance: for if one brother of the halfe bloud dye, the admi-
5. Ed. 6. Adm. 47. niſtration ought to bee committed to his other brother of the halfe bloud, if there bee no neerer by the father.

33. H. 6. 55. So if the vncle by the mother be attainted, and pardoned, and land deſcend from the father to the ſonne within age held in ſoccage, the vncle ſhall be guardian in ſoccage; for that ſauoureth ſo little of the priuity of heire, as the poſſibility to inherit ſhutteth not.

But if a Feme tenant intaile aſſent to the rauiſher, and haue no iſſue, and her couſin is attainted, and pardoned, and purchaſeth the reuerſion,
5. Ed. 4. 5. hee ſhall not enter for a forfeiture. For though the law giueth it not in point of inheritance, but onely as a perquiſite to any of the bloud ſo hee bee next in eſtate, yet the recompence is vnderſtood for the ſtaine of his bloud, which cannot bee conſidered when it is once wholly corrupted before.

So

So if a villein bee attainted, yet the Lord ſhall haue the iſſues of his villein borne before or after the attainder; for the Lord hath them *Iure naturæ* but as the increaſe of a flocke.

Quære whether if the eldeſt ſonne bee attainted, and pardoned, the Lord ſhall haue aide of his tenants to make him a Knight, and it ſeemeth hee ſhall; for the words of the writ hath *filium primogenitum*, and not *filium & hæredem*, and the like writ hath *pur file marrier* who is no heire. F. N. br. 82 9. Regiſter. fol. 87.

Receditur à placitis iuris, potius quam iniuriæ, & delicta maneant impunita. Regula 12.

THe law hath many grounds and poſitiue learnings, which are not of the maximes and concluſions of reaſon, but yet are learnings receiued with the law, ſet downe, and will not haue called in queſtion: theſe may bee rather called *placita iuris* than *regulæ iuris*, with ſuch maximes the law will diſpenſe, rather than crimes and wrongs ſhould bee vnpuniſhed, *quia ſalus populi ſuprema lex*, and *ſalus populi* is contained in the repreſſing offences by puniſhment.

Therefore if an aduouſon be graunted to two, and the heires of one of them, and an vſurpation bee had, they both ſhall ioine in a writ of right of aduouſon; and yet it is a ground in law, that a writ

writ of right lieth of no lesse estate than a fee-simple; but because the tenant for life hath no other seuerall action in the law giuen him, and also that the iointure is not broken, and so the tenant in fee-simple cannot bring his writ of right alone, therefore rather than hee shall bee depriued wholly of remedy, and this wrong vnpunished, hee shall ioine his companion with him, notwithstanding the feeblenesse of his estate.

46. Ed. 3. 21. But if lands bee giuen to two, and to the heires of one of them, and they leese in a *Precipe* by default, now they shall not ioine in a writ of right, because the tenant for life hath a seuerall action, *viz.* a *quod ei deforciat*, in which respect the iointure is broken.

So if tenant for life and his lessor ioine in a lease for yeares, and the lessee commit waste, they shall ioine in punishing this waste, and *locus vastatus* shall goe to the tenant for life, and the damages to him in reuersion, and yet an action of waste lieth not for tenant for life, but because hee in the reuersion cannot haue it alone, because of the meane estate for life, therefore rather than the waste shall bee vnpunished, they shall ioine.

45. Ed. 3. 3.
22. H. 6. 24. So if two coperceners bee, and they lease the land, and one of them dye, and hath issue, and the lessee commit waste, the aunt and the issue shall ioine in punishing this waste, and the issue shall

recouer

recouer the moity of the place wasted, and the aunt the other moity and the entire damages; and yet *actio iniuriarum moritur cum persona*, but *in fauorabilibus magis attenditur quod prodest, quàm quod nocet.*

So if a man recouers by erroneous iudgement, and hath issue two daughters, and one of them is attainted, the writ of error shall bee brought against the parceners, notwithstanding the priuity faile in the one. 20.Ed.2. F. discent. 16.

Also it is a positiue ground, that the accessary in felony cannot bee proceeded against vntill the principall bee tryed; yet if a man vpon subtilty and malice set a mad man by some deuice to kill him, and hee doth so, now forasmuch as the mad man is excused, because hee can haue no will, nor malice, the law accounteth the incitor as principall, though hee bee absent, rather than the crime shall goe vnpunished. 33. Eliz.

So it is a ground of the law, that the appeale of murther goeth not to the heire where the party murthered hath a wife, nor to the younger brother where there is an elder; yet if the wife murther her husband, because shee is the party offendor, the appeale leaps ouer to the heire; and so if the sonne and heire murther his father, it goeth to the second brother. Fitz. Corone. 47. Ed. 4. M. 28.6. Stamff. lib. 2. fol. 60.

But

But if the rule bee one of the higher sort of maximes, that are *regulæ rationales* and not *positiuæ*, then the law will rather endure a particular offence to escape without punishment, than violate such a rule.

As it is a rule that penall statutes shall not bee taken by equity, and the statute of 1. *Ed. 6.* enacts that those that are attainted for stealing of horses shall not haue their Cleargy, the Iudges conceiued, that this did not extend to him that should steale but one horse, and therefore procured a new act for it in 2. *Ed. 6. cap.* 33. and they had reason for it, as I take the law, for it is not like the case vpon the statute of *Glost.* that giues the action of waste against him that holds *pro termino vitæ vel annorum*. It is true, that if a man holds but for a yeare, he is within the statute, for it is to bee noted, that penall statutes are taken strictly and literally onely in the point of defining and setting downe the fact and the punishment, & in those clauses that doe concerne them, and not generally in words that are but circumstances and conueyance in the putting of the case, and so see the diuersity; for if the law bee, that for such an offence a man shall leese his right hand, and the offendor hath had his right hand before cut off in the warres, hee shall not lose his left hand, but the crime shall rather passe without the punishment which the law assigned, than the

Plow. 467.

Lit. cap.
46. Ed. 3. 31.

the letter of the law ſhould bee extended; but if the ſtatute of 1. *Ed.* 6. had beene, that hee that ſhould ſteale one horſe ſhould bee ouſted of his Cleargie, then there had beene no queſtion at all but if a man had ſtolne more horſes than one, but that hee had beene within the ſtatute, *quia omne maius continet in ſe minus.*

Non accipi debent verba in demonſtrationem falſam quæ competunt in limitationem veram. Regula 13.

THough falſitie of addition or demonſtration doth not hurt where you giue the thing a proper name, yet neuertheleſſe if it ſtand doubtfull vpon the words, whether they import a falſe reference and demonſtration, or whether they be words of reſtaint that limit the generality of the former name, the law will neuer intend error or falſehood.

Therefore if the Pariſh of Hurſt do extend into 12.Eliz. 6.29 the Counties of Wiltſh. and Barkſh. and I graunt 23.Eliz.Dyer 376. my Cloſe called Callis, ſituate and lying in the 7.Ed.6.Dy.56. Pariſh of Hurſt in the countie of Wiltſh. and the troth is, that the whole Cloſe lieth in the County of Barkſh. yet the law is, that it paſſeth well enough, becauſe there is a certaintie ſufficient in that I haue giuen it a proper name which the falſe reference doth not deſtroy, and not vpon the reaſon that theſe words, in the Countie of Wiltſh.

Wiltsh. shall be taken to goe to the Parish onely, and so to bee true in some sort, and not to the Close, and so to be false. For if I had graunted *omnes terras meas in Parochia de Hurst in Com. Wiltsh.* and I had no lands in Wiltsh. but in Barksh. nothing had past.

9.Ed.4.7. 21.Ed.3.18. 28.Eliz. But in the principall case, if the Close called Callis had extended part into Wiltsh. and part into Barksh. then onely that part had passed which lay in Wiltsh.

29.Reg. So if I graunt *omnes & singulas terras meas in tenura I. D. quas perquesiui de I. N. in Indentura dimimissionis fact' I. B. specificat.* If I haue land wherein some of these references are true and the rest false, and no land wherein they are all true, nothing passeth: as if I haue land in the tenure of I. D. and purchased of I N. but not specified in the Indenture to I. B. or if I haue land which purchased of I. N. and specified in the Indenture of demise to I B. and not in the tenure of I.D.

But if I haue some land wherin all these demonstrations are true, and some wherin part of them are true and part false, then shal they be intended words of true limitation to passe only those lands wherein all those circumstances are true.

Regula 24. *Licet dispositio de interesse futuro sit inutilis, tamen potest fieri declaratio praecedens quae sortiatur effectum interueniente nouo actu.*

The

THe law doth not allow of grants except there be a foundatiõ of an interest in the grantor; for the law that will not accept of graunts of titles or of things in action which are imperfect interests, much lesse will it allow a man to graunt or incumber that which is no interest at all but meerely future.

But of declarations precedent before any interest vested, the law doth allow but with this difference, so that there be some new act or conueiance to giue life & vigour to the declaratiõ precedent.

Now the best rule of distinctio between graunts & declarations, is, that graunts are neuer countermandable not in respect of the nature of the conueiance or instrument, though somtime in respect of the interest granted they are, wheras declarations euermore are countermãdable in their natures

And therefore if I graunt vnto you, that if you enter into an obligation to me of 100 l. and after doe procure mee such a lease, that then the same obligation shall be void, and you enter into such an obligation vnto me, & afterwards do procure such a lease, yet the obligation is simple, because the defeisance was made of that which was not. 20.Eliz. 19.H.6.63.

So if I graunt vnto you a rent charge out of white acre and that it shall be lawfull for you to distraine in all my other lands wherof I am now seised, and which I shall hereafter purchase, although 27.Ed.3

though this bee but a libertie of distresse, and no rent saue onely out of white acre, yet as to the lands afterwards to bee purchased the clause is voyd.

29.Ed.3.6. 24.Eliz. So if a reuersion bee graunted to I.S. and I.D. a stranger by his deede doe graunt to I.S. that if he purchase the particular estate, hee will atturne to the graunt, this is a void atturnment, notwithstanding hee doth afterwards purchase the particular estate.

13.14. Eliz. 20.21.Eliz. 25.Eliz. But of declarations the law is contrarie; as if the disseisee make a charter of feoffement to I.S. and a letter of atturney to enter and make liuery and seisme, and deliuer the deede of feoffement, and afterwards liuerie and seisme is made accordingly, this is a good feoffement and yet hee had no other thing than a right at the time of the deliuerie of the charter, but because a deede of feoffement is but matter of declaration and euidence, and there is a new act which is M 38.& 39.Eliz. the liuerie subsequent, therfore it is good in law.

So if a man make a feoffement to I.S. vpon condition to enfeoffe I. N. within certaine daies, 36.Eliz. and there are deedes made both of the first feoffement and the second, and letters of atturney accordingly, and both those deedes of feoffement, and letters of atturney are deliuered at a time, so that the second deede of feoffement and

and letters of atturny are deliuered when the first feoffee had nothing in the land, and yet if both liueries bee made accordingly, all is good.

So if I couenant with I. S by indenture, that before such a day I will purchase the mannour of D. and before the same day I will leuy a fine of the same land, and that the same fine shall bee to certaine vses which I expresse in the same indenture, this indenture to leud vses being but matter of declaration and countermandable, at my pleasure will suffice, though the land be purchased after; because there is a new act to bee done, *viz.* the fine.

But if there were no new act then otherwise it is; as if I couenant with my sonne, in considera- tion of naturall loue, to stand seised vnto his vse of the lands which I shall afterwards purchase, yet the vse is voide; and the reason is, because there is no new act, nor transmutation of possession following to perfect this inception; for the vse must bee limited by the feoffor, and not the feoffee, and hee had nothing at the time of the couenant.

25. Eliz. 27. Eliz.

So if I deuise the mannour of D. by speciall name, of which at that time I am not seised, and after I purchase it, except I make some new publication of my will this deuice is voide; and the reason is, because that my death which is the con-

Com. Plowd. Rigdens case.

consummation of my will is the act of God, and not my act, and therefore no such act as the law requireth.

But if I grant vnto I. S. authority by my deed to demise for yeares, the land whereof I am now seised, or hereafter shall bee seised; and after I purchase the lands, and I. S. my Atturney doth demise them, this is a good demise, because the demise of my atturney is a new act, and all one with a demise by my selfe.

21. Eliz. But if I morgage land, and after couenant with I. S. in consideration of money which I receiue of him, that after I haue entred for the condition broken, I will stand seised to the vse of the same I. S. and I enter, and this deede is enrolled, and all within the six months, yet nothing passeth away, because this enrollment is no new act, but a perfectiue ceremony of the first deede of bargaine and sale; and the law is more strong in that case, because of the vehement relation which the enrollment hath to the time of the bargaine and sale, at what time hee had nothing but a naked condition.

5. Ed. 6. Br. So if two Iointments bee, and one of them bargaine, and sell the whole land, and before the enrollment his companion dieth, nothing passeth of the moity accrued vnto him by suruiuor.

In

In criminalibus sufficit generalis malitia intentionis cum facto paris gradus. Regula 15.

ALl crimes haue their conception in a corrupt intent, and haue their consummation and issuing in some particular fact; which though it bee not the fact at which the intention of the malefactor leuelled, yet the law giueth him no aduantage of that error, if another particular ensue of as high a nature.

Therefore if an impoisoned apple bee laid in a place to poison I. S. and I. D. commeth by chance and eateth it, this is murther in the principall that is actor, and yet the malice *in indiuiduo* was not against I. D. 18. Eliz. Sanders case com. 474.

So if a thiefe finde the doore open, and come in by night and rob an house, and bee taken with the manner, and breake a doore to escape, this is burglary, yet the breaking of the doore was without any felonious intent, but it is one entire act. Cr. I. peace. 30.

So if a Caliuer bee discharged with a murtherous intent at I. S. and the Peece breake, and strike into the eye of him that dischargeth it and killeth him, hee is *felo de se*, and yet his intention was not to hurt himselfe; for *felonia de se* and murther are *crimina paris gradus*. For if a man perswade another to kill himselfe, and bee Casu.

present

present when hee doth so, hee is a murtherer.

Cr.Inst.peace. fol.18.19. But *quare*, if I. S. lay impoisoned fruit for some other stranger his enemy, and his father or mother come and eate it, whether this bee petty treason, because it is not altogether *crimen paris gradus*.

Regula 16. *Mandata licita recipiunt strictam interpretationem, sed illicita latam & extensam.*

IN commiting of lawful authoritie to another a man may limit it as strictly as it pleaseth him, and if the partie authorized doe transgresse his authoritie, though it bee but in circumstance expressed, it shall be void in the whole act.

But when a man is author and monitor to another to commit an vnlawfull act, then he shall not excuse himselfe by circumstances not pursued.

10.H.7.19.15. 16. 16.El.Dy.337. Therefore if I make a letter of atturney to I.S. to deliuer liuerie and seisin in the capitall Messuage, and hee doth it in another place of the land, or betweene the houres of 2. and 3. and he doth it after or before; or if I make a Charter of 16.El.Dy.337. 11.El.Dy.283. 38.H.8.68.Dy. feoffement to I.D. and I.B. and expresse the seisin to be deliuered to I. D. and my atturney deliuer it to I. B. in all these cases the act of the atturney as as to execute the estate, is void; but if I say generally to I. D. whom I meane onely to enfeoffe, and my atturney make it to his atturney, it shall be intended, for it is a livery to him in law.

But on the other side, If a man command I.S. to robbe I. D. on Shooters-hill, and hee doth it on Gads-hill, or to robbe him such a day, and he doth it not himselfe but procureth I. B. to do it; or to kill him by poison, and hee doth it by violence; in all these cases notwithstanding the fact bee not executed, yet hee is accessary neverthelesse. 18. El. Sanders case. Com. 475.

But if it be to kill I.S. and he killeth I.D. mistaking him for I.S. then the acts are distant in substance, and he is not accessary. Ibidem.

And be it that the facts be of differing degrees, and yet of a kinde,

As if a man bid I. S. to pilfer away such things out of a house, and precisely restraine him to doe it sometimes when he is gotten in without breaking of the house, and yet hee breaketh the house, yet hee is accessary to the burglarie: for a man cannot condition with an vnlawfull act, but he must at his perill take heede how hee putteth himselfe into another mans hands.

But if a man bid one robbe I. S. as he goeth to

18.Eliz.in Sanders case. pl.Com.475. Sturbridge-faire, and he robbe him in his house the variance seemes to be of substance, and he is not accessarie.

Regula 17. *De fide & officio Iudicis non recipitur quæstio, sed de scientia, siue error sit Iuris siue facti.*

THe law doth so much respect the certainetie of iudgement, and the credit and authoritie of Iudges, as it will not permit any error to bee assigned that impeacheth them in their trust and office, and in wilfull abuse of the same, but only in ignorance, and mistaking either of the law or of the case and matter in fact.

F. N.br.fol. 21. 7. H.7.4. And therefore if I will assigne for error, that whereas the verdict passed for me, the Court receiued it contrary, and so gaue iudgement against me, this shall not be accepted.

3.H.6.ass.3. So if I will alledge for errour, that whereas I. S. offered to plead a sufficient barre, the Court refused it, and draue me from it, this errour shall not be allowed.

2.M.Dy.114. But the greatest doubt is where the Court doth determine of the veritie of the matter in fact; so that is rather a point of tryall than a point of iudgement,

iudgement, whether it shall bee re-examined in errour.

As if an appeale of Maihem bee brought, and the Court, by the assistance of the Chirurgians adiudge it to bee a Maihem, whether the partie grieued may bring a writ of error, and I hold the Law to be he cannot. 1.Mar.5. 28.ass.pl.15. 21.H.7.40.33.

So if one of the Prothonotaries of the Common pleas bring an assize of his office, and alleage fees belonging to the same office in certaintie and issue is taken vpon these fees, this issue shall be tried by the Iudges by way of examination, and if they determine it for the plaintiffe, and he haue iudgement to recouer arrerages accordingly, the defendant can bring no writ of errour of this iudgement, though the fees in troth be other. 8.H.4.3. 1.Mar. Dy. 89. 5.Mar.Dy.163.

So if a woman bring a writ of dower, and the tenaunt plead her husband was aliue, this shall bee tried by proofes and not by iurie, and vpon iudgement giuen on either side no error lies. 8.H.6.23. 2.El.285.Dy. 43.ass.26. 41.ass.5. 39.ass.9.

So if *nul tiel record* be pleaded which is to bee tried by the inspection of the record, and iudgement be thereupon giuen, no error lieth. 5.Ed.4.3. 9.H.7.2. 19.H.6.52.

So if in the assize the tenant saith, he is *Countee de dale & nient nosme Countee*, in the writ this 22.ass.pl.24. 19.Ed.4.6.

 shall

ſhall bee tried by the records of the Chancerie, and vpon iudgement giuen no errour lieth.

So if a felon demaund his cleargy, and read well and diſtinctly, and the Court who is iudge thereof doe put him from his cleargie wrongfully, errour ſhall neuer bee brought vpon this attainder.

9. Aſſ. 8. F. N. Br. 21. So if vpon iudgement giuen vpon confeſsion for default, and the Court doe aſſeſſe damages, the defendant ſhall neuer bring a writ, though the damage bee outragious.

And it ſeemeth in the caſe of maihem, and ſome other caſes, that the Court may diſmiſſe themſelues of diſcuſſing the matter by examination, and put it to a Iury, and then the party grieued ſhall haue his attaint; and therefore it ſeemeth that the Court that doth depriue a man of his action, ſhould bee ſubiect to an action; but that, notwithſtanding, the law will not haue, as was ſaid in the beginning, the Iudges called in queſtion in the point of their office when they vndertake to diſcuſſe the iſſue, and that is the true reaſon; for to ſay that the reaſon of theſe caſes ſhould bee, becauſe tryall by the Court ſhould bee peremptorie as tryall by certificate, (as by the Biſhop in caſe of baſtardy, or by the Marſhall of the King &c.) the caſes are nothing alike; for the reaſon of thoſe caſes of certificate is,

21. Aſſ. 24. 11. H. 4. 41. 7. H. 6. 37.

is, becauſe if the Court ſhould not giue credit to the certificate, but ſhould re-examin it, they haue no other meane but to write againe to the ſame Lord Biſhop, or the ſame Lord Marſhall, which were friuolous, becauſe it is not to bee preſumed they would differ from their former certificate; whereas in theſe other caſes of error the matter is drawne before a ſuperiour Court, to re-examine the errors of an inferiour Court: and therfore the true reaſon, as was ſaid, that to examine againe that which the Court had tryed, were in ſubſtance to attaint the Court.

And therefore this is a certaine rule in error, that error in law is euer of ſuch matters as were not croſſed by the record, as to alledge the death of the tenant at the time of the iudgement giuen, nothing appeareth vpon record to the contrarie.

So when the infant leuies a fine, it appeareth not vpon the record that hee is an infant, therefore it is an error in fact, and ſhall bee tried by inſpection during nonage. F. N. Br. 21.

But if a writ of error bee brought in the Kings Bench, of a fine leuied by an infant, and the Court by inſpection and examination doth affirme the fine, the infant, though it bee during his infancy, ſhall neuer bring a writ of error in the Parliament vpon this iudgement; not but that error lies after error, but becauſe it doth now ap- 2. R. 3. 20.

peare

peare vpon the record that he is now of full age, therefore it can bee no error in fact. And therefore if a man will assigne for error that fact, that whereas the Iudges gaue iudgement for him, the Clerkes entred it in the roll against him, this error shall not bee allowed, and yet it doth not touch the Iudges but the Clerkes; but the reason is, if it bee an error, it is an error in fact; and you shall neuer alledge an error in fact contrary to the record.

F. N. Br. 21.

9. Ed. 4. 3.

Regula 18.

Persona coniuncta æquiparatur interesse proprio.

THe law hath that respect of nature and coniunction of bloud, as in diuers cases it compareth and matcheth neerenesse of bloud with consideration of profit and interest, yea, and in some cases alloweth of it more strongly.

7. & 8. Eliz.

Therefore if a man couenant in consideration of bloud, to stand seised to the vse of his brother, or sonne, or neere kinsman, an vse is well raised of this couenant without transmutation of possession; neuerthelesse it is true, that consideration of bloud is not to ground a personall contract vpon: as if I contract with my sonne, that in consideration of bloud I will giue vnto him such a summe of mony, this is a *nudum pactum*, and no *assumpsit* lieth vpon it; for to subiect mee to an action,

action, there needeth a consideration of benefit, but the vse the law raiseth without suite or action; and besides, the law doth match reall considerations with reall agreements and couenants.

So if a suite bee commenced against mee, my 19.Ed.4.9.
sonne, or brother, I may maintaine aswell as hee 19.Ed.4.22. 22.H.6.35.
in remainder for his interest, or his Lawyer for 21.H.6.15.16.
his fee, and if my brother haue a suite against my 22.H.6.5. 20.H.6.
nephew or cousin, yet it is at my election to 14.H.6.6.
maintaine the cause of my nephew or cousin, 14.H.7.2.
though the aduerse party bee neerer vnto mee in bloud.

So in challenges of Iuries, challenge of bloud 14.&15.Eliz.
is as good as challenge within distresse, and it is 21.Ed.4.75. Com.425.
not materiall how farre off the kindred bee, so the pedegree can bee conueyed in a certainty whether it bee of the halfe bloud or whole.

So if a man menace mee, that hee will impri- 15.H.6.17.
son, or hurt in body my father, or my childe, ex- 39 H.6.50. 21.Ed.4.13.
cept I make such an obligation, I shall auoide 18.H.6.21.
this duresse, as well as if the duresse had beene to 15.Ed.4.1.
mine owne person: and yet if a man menace me, by taking away or destruction of my goods, this
is no good duresse to pleade, and the reason is, 39.H.6.51.
because the law can make mee reparation of that 7.Ed.4.21.
losse, and so it cannot of the other. 20.Ass.14.

So if a man vnder the yeares of 21. contract

M for

Perk.4. D. cap. 28.

for the nursing of his lawfull childe; this contract is good, and shall not bee auoided by infancy no more than if hee had contracted for his owne aliments or erudition.

Regula 19. *Non impedit clausula derogatoria, quo minus ab eadem potestate res dissoluantur a quibus constituuntur.*

ACts which are in their natures reuocable cannot by strength of words be fixed or perperpetuated, yet men haue put in vre two meanes to binde themselues from changing or dissoluing that which they haue set downe, whereof one is *clausula derogatoria*, the other *interpositio iuramenti*, whereof the former is onely pertinent to this present purpose.

This *clausula derogatoria* is by the common practicall terme called *clausula non obstante de futuro esse*, the one weakening and disanulling any matter past to the contrarie, the other any matter to come, and this latter is that only whereof we speake.

The *Clausula de non obstante de futuro*, the law iudgeth to be idle and of no force, because it doth depriue men of that which of all other things is most incident to humane condition, and that is alteration or repentance.

Therefore

Therefore if I make my will, and in the end thereof doe adde ſuch like clauſe, [Alſo my will is if I ſhall reuoke this preſent will, or declare any new will, except the ſame ſhall bee in writing, ſubſcribed with the hands of two witneſſes, that ſuch reuocation or new declaration ſhall be vtterly void, and by theſe preſents I doe declare the ſame not to bee my will, but this my former will to ſtand] any ſuch pretended will to the contrarie notwithſtanding; yet neuertheleſſe this clauſe or any the like neuer ſo exactly penned, and although it do reſtraine the reuocation but in circumſtance and not altogether, is of no force or efficacie to fortifie the former will againſt the ſecond, but I may by paroll without writing repeale the ſame will, and make a new.

So if there bee a ſtatute made that no Sheriffe ſhall continue in his office aboue a yeare, and if any Pattent be made to the contrarie, it ſhall bee voide, and if there be any *Clauſula de non obſtante* contained in ſuch Pattent to diſpence with this preſent act, that ſuch clauſe alſo ſhall be void; yet neuertheleſſe a Pattent of the Sheriffes office made by the King with a *non obſtante* will bee good in law, contrary to ſuch ſtatute, which pretendeth to exclude *non obſtantes*, and the reaſon is, becauſe it is an inſeparable prerogatiue of the Crowne to diſpence with politicke ſtatutes and of that kinde, and then the derogatory clauſe hurteth not.

28.Ed.3.cap.7.
24.Ed.3. cap.9.
2.H.7.6.

So if an act of Parlament bee made wherein there is a clause contained, that it shall not bee lawfull for the King by authoritie of Parliament during the space of seuen yeares to repeale and determine the same act, this is a void clause, and such act may be repealed within the seuen yeares, and yet if the Parliament should enact in the nature of the ancient *Lex Regia*, that there should bee no more Parliaments held, but that the King should haue the authoritie of the Parlament; this act were good in Law, *quia potestas suprema seipsum dissoluere potest, legare non potest*: for as it is in the power of a man to kill a man, but it is not in his power to saue him aliue and to restraine him from breathing or feeling; so it is in the power of a Parliament to extinguish or transfer their own authoritie, but not whilst the authoritie remaines entire to restraine the functions and exercises of the same authoritie.

So in the 28. of K.H.8. chap. 17. there was a statute made, that all acts that passed in the minority of Kings, reckoning the same vnder the years of 24. might be annulled and reuoked by their letters patents when they came to the same years; but this act in the first of K.Ed.6. who was then between the years of 10. & 11. ca. 11. was repealed, and a new law surrogate in place thereof, wherein a more reasonable libertie was giuen: and wherein, though other lawes are made reuocable according to the prouision of the former law with

24.El.Dy.313.
P.Com.563.

with ſome new forme preſcribed, yet that verie Law of reuocation, together with pardons, is made irreuocable and perpetuall ; ſo that there is a direct contrarietie betweene theſe two lawes : for if the former ſtands, which maketh all latter lawes during the minoritie of Kings reuocable without exception of anie law whatſoeuer, then that very law of repeale is concluded in the generalitie, and ſo it ſelfe made reuocable : on the other ſide, that law making no doubt of the abſolute repeale of the firſt law, though it ſelfe were made during the minoritie, which was the verie caſe of the former law in the new prouiſion which it maketh, hath a preciſe exception, that the law of repeale ſhall not be repealed.

But the law is, that the firſt law by the impertinency of it was void *ab initio & ipſo facto* without repeale, as if a law were made, that no new ſtatute ſhould be made during 7. yeares, and the ſame ſtatute be repealed within the 7. yeares, if the firſt ſtatute ſhould bee good, then the repeale could not bee made thereof within that time ; for the law of repeale were a new law, and that were diſabled by the former law, therefore it is void in it ſelfe, and the rule holds, *perpetua lex eſt nullam legem humanam ac poſitiuam perpetuam eſſe, & clauſula quæ abrogationem excludit initio non valet.*

Neither is the difference of the ciuill law ſo

reaſonable as colourable, for they diſtinguiſh and ſay that a derogatorie clauſe is good to diſable any latter act, except you reuoke the ſame clauſe before you proceed to eſtabliſh any later diſpoſition, or declaration; for they ſay, that *clauſula derogatoria ad alias ſequentes voluntates poſita in teſtamento (viz. ſi teſtator dicat qd' ſi contigerit eum facere aliud teſtamentum non vult illud valere) operatur quod ſequens diſpoſitio ab ipſa clauſula reguletur & per conſequens quod ſequens diſpoſitio duretur ſine voluntate & ſic quod non ſit attendendum.* The ſenſe is, that where a former will is made, and after a later will, the reaſon why without an expreſſe reuocation of the former will it is by implication reuoked, is becauſe of the repugnancie betweene the diſpoſition of the former and the later.

But where there is ſuch a derogatorie clauſe, there can bee gathered no ſuch repugnancy, becauſe it ſeemeth that the teſtator had a purpoſe at the making of the firſt will to make ſome ſhew of a new will, which neuertheleſſe his intention was ſhould not take place: but this was anſwered before; for if that clauſe were allowed to be good vntill a reuocation, then would no reuocation at all be made, therefore it muſt needs be void by operation of law at firſt. Thus much of *Clauſula derogatoria.*

Actus inceptus cuius perfectio pendet ex voluntate partium reuocari potest, si autem pendet ex voluntate tertiæ personæ vel ex contigenti non potest. Regula 28.

IN acts that are fully executed and consummate, the law makes this difference, that if the first parties haue put it in the power of a third person, or of a contigency, to giue a perfection to their acts, then they haue put it out of their owne reach and liberty; therefore there is no reason they should reuoke them: but if the consummation depend vpon the same consent, which was the inception, then the law accounteth it in vaine to restraine them from reuoking of it, for as they may frustrate it by omission, and *non feisance*, at a certaine time or in a certaine sort, or circumstance, so the law permitteth them to dissolue it by an expresse consent, before that time, or without that circumstance.

Therefore if two exchange land by deede, or without deede, and neither enter, they may make a reuocation or dissolution of the same exchange by mutuall consent, so it bee by deede, but not by paroll, for as much as the making of an exchange needeth no deede, because it is to be perfected by entry, which is a ceremony notorious in the nature of a liuerie; but it cannot bee dissolued but by deede, because it dischargeth that which is but title. F. N. Br. 36. 13. H. 7. 13. 14.

solued

F.36.Eliz. So if I contract with I. D. that if hee lay mee into my seller three tunnes of wine before Mich. that I will bring into his Garner 20. quarters of wheat before Christmas, before either of these daies the parties may by assent dissolue the contract; but after the first day there is a perfection giuen to the contract by action on the one side, and they may make crosse releases by deede or paroll, but neuer dissolue the contract; for there is a difference betweene dissoluing the contract and release or surrender of the thing contracted for: as if lessee for 20. yeares make a lease for 10. yeares, and after he take a lease for 5. yeares, yet this cannot inure by way of surrender: for a pettie lease deriued out of a greater cannot bee surrendred backe againe, but inureth onely by dissolution of contract; for a lease of land is but a contract executorie from time to time of the profits of the land, to arise as a man may sell his corn or his tythe to spring or to be perceiued for diuers future yeares.

But to return from our digression, on the other side, if I contract with you for cloath at such a price as I.S. shall name; there if I.S. refuse to name, the contract is void, but the parties cannot discharge it, because they haue put it in the power of the third person to perfect.

11.H.7.19. 1.R.2. F.atturment.8. So if I graunt my reuersion, though this be an imperfect act before atturnement, yet because the

attturnatturnment is the act of a stranger, this is not simply reuokable, but by a policie or circumstance in law, as by leuying a fine, or making a bargaine and sale, or the like.

So if I present a Clerke to the Bishop, now can I not reuoke this presentation, because I haue put it out of my selfe, that is the Bishop by admission to perfect my act begunne. 31.Ed.1.F.Q Imp.185. 14.Ed.4.2. 38.Ed.3.35.

The same difference appeareth in nominations and elections; as if I enfeoffe such a one as I. D. shall name within a yeare, and I. D. name I. B. yet before the feoffement and within the yeare I. D. may countermand his nomination and name againe, because no interest passeth out of him. But if I enfeoffe I. S. to the vse of such a one as I. D. shall name within a yeare, then if I D. name I B. it is not reuocable, because the vse passeth presently by operation of law. 14.Ed.4.2.

So in iudiciall acts the rule of the ciuill law holdeth, *sententia interlocutoria reuocari potest*; that is, that an order may be reuoked, but a iudgement cannot; and the reason is, because there is a title of execution or barre giuen presently vnto the partie vpon iudgement, and so it is out of the Iudge to reuoke in Courts ordered by the common law.

Regula 21. *Clausula vel dispositio inutilis per presumptionem remotam vel causam, ex post facto non fulcitur.*

C*Lausula vel dispositio inutilis* are said, when the act or the words doe worke or expresse no more than the law by intendment would haue supplied; and therefore the doubling or iterating of that and no more, which the conceit of law doth in a sort preuent and preoccupate, is reputed nugation, and is not supported and made of substance either by a forreine intendment of some purpose, in regard whereof it might bee materiall, nor vpon any cause emerging afterwards, which may induce an operation of those idle words.

32.H.8. Goord. 39. Ber. 2. M. Br. deuises 41. And therefore if a man demise land at this day to his sonne and heire, this is a voide deuise, because the disposition of law did cast the same vpon the heire by descent, and yet if it be Knights seruice land, and the heire within age, if hee take by the deuise hee shall haue two parts of the profits to his owne vse, and the guardian shall haue benefit but of the third; but if a man deuise land to his two daughters, hauing no sonnes, then the deuise is good, because hee doth alter the disposition of law, for by the law they shall take in 29.H.8. Dy.22. copercenarie, but by the deuise they shall take iointly, and this is not any forreine collaterall purpose, but in point of taking of estate.

So

So if a man make a feoffement in fee, to the vſe of his laſt will and teſtament, theſe words of ſpeciall limitation are voide, and the law reſerueth the ancient vſe to the feoffor and his heires: and yet if the words might ſtand, then might it bee authority by his will to declare and appoint vſes, & then though it were Knights ſeruice land, hee might diſpoſe the whole. As if a man make a feoffement in fee, to the vſe of the will and teſtament of a ſtranger, there the ſtranger may declare an vſe of the whole by his will, notwithſtanding it bee Knights ſeruice land, but the reaſon of the principall caſe is, becauſe vſes before the ſtatute of 27. *H.* 8. were to haue beene diſpoſed by will, and therefore before that ſtatute an vſe limited in the forme aforeſaid, was but a friuolous limitation, in regard of the old vſe that the law reſerued was deuiſable; and the ſtatute of 27. altereth not the law, as to the creating and limiting of any vſe, and therefore after that ſtatute, and before the ſtatute of wills, when no land could haue beene deuiſed, yet was it a voide limitation as before, and ſo continueth to this day. 19. H. 8. 11. 5. Ed. 4. 8.

But if I make a feoffement in fee, to the vſe of my laſt will and teſtament, thereby to declare an eſtate taile and no greater eſtate; and after my death and after ſuch eſtate declared ſhall expire, or in default of ſuch declaration then to the vſe of I. S. and his heires, this is a good limitation,

19.H.8.11. 6.Ed.4.8. and I may by my will declare an vse of the whole land to a stranger, though it bee held in knights seruice, and yet I haue an estate in fee simple by vertue of the old vse during life.

32.H.8.43.Dy. 20.H.8.8.Dyer. 7.Eliz.237.Dy. So if I make a feoffement in fee to the vse of my right heires, this is a void limitation and the vse reserued by the law doth take place, and yet if the limitation should be good the heire should come in by way of purchase, who otherwise commeth in by descent, but this is but a circumstance which the law respecteth not, as was proued before.

But if I make a feoffement in fee to the vse of 10.El.274.Dy. my right heires, and the right heires of I.S. this is a good vse, because I haue altered the disposition of law; neither is it void for a moitie, but both our right heires when they come in beeing shall 2.Ed.3.29. 30.E.1.Fitz. Deuise.9. take by ioint purchase, and hee to whom the first falleth shall take the whole subiect, neuerthelesse to his companions titles, so it haue not descended from the first heire to the heire of the heire: for a man cannot bee ioint tenant claiming by purchase, and the other by descent, because they be seuerall titles.

So if a man hauing land on the part of his Mother make a feoffement in fee to the vse of himselfe and his heires, this vse though expressed, shall not goe to him and the heires of the part of his

his Father as a new purchase, no more than it should haue done if it had beene a feoffement in fee nakedly without consideration, for the intendment is remote. But if baron and feme bee, and they ioine in a fine of the femes land and expresse an vse to the husband and wife and their heires: this limitation shall giue a ioint estate by intierties to them both, because the intendment of law would haue conueied the vse to the feme alone. And thus much touching forreine intendments. 4.M.133. pl.6.Dyer. 5.Ed.4.8. 19.H.8.11.

For matter *ex post facto*, if a lease for life bee made to two, and the suruiuor of them, and they after make partition: now these words (and the suruiuor of them) should seeme to carry purpose as a limitation, that either of them should bee stated of his part for both their liues seuerally; but yet the law at the first construeth the words but words of dilating to describe a ioint estate; and if one of them dye after partition there shall bee no occupant, but his part shall reuert. 30.ass.8.Fitz. part.16. 31.H.8.46. p.7.D.

So if a man graunt a rent charge out of 10. acres, and grant further that the whole rent shall issue out of euerie acre, and distresse accordingly, & afterwards the grauntee purchase an acre: now this clause should seeme to be material to vphold the rent; but yet neuerthelesse the law at first accepteth of these words but as words of explanation, and then notwithſtanding the whole rent is extinct.

So if a gift intaile be made vpon condition, that if tenaunt intaile die without iſſue it ſhall be lawfull for the donor to enter and the donee diſcontinue and die without iſſue: now this condition ſhould ſeeme materiall to giue him benefit of entrie, but becauſe it did at the firſt limit the eſtate according to the limitation of law, it worketh nothing vpon this matter emergent afterward.

4.E.6.Com.33. per Hinde. 27.H.8.6.

So if a gift intaile bee made of lands held in Knights ſeruice with an expreſſe reſeruation of the ſame ſeruice, whereby the land is held ouer, and the gift is with warrantie, and the land is euicted, and other land recouered in value againſt the donor held in ſoccage, now the tenure which the law makes betweene the donor and donee ſhall be in ſoccage, and not in knights ſeruice, becauſe the firſt reſeruation was according to the oweltie of ſeruice, which was no more than the law would haue reſerued.

22.Aſſ.pl.52.

But if a gift intaile had beene made of lands held in ſoccage with a reſeruation of knights ſeruice tenure, and with warrantie, then becauſe the intendment of law is altered the new land ſhall be held by the ſame ſeruice the laſt land was, without any regard at all to the tenure paramount:

mount: and thus much of matter *ex post facto*.

This Rule faileth where that the law saith as much as the partie, but vpon forreine matter not pregnant and appearing vpon the same act, and conueiance, as if lessee for life be, and hee lets for 20. yeares, if he liue so long; this limitation (if he liue so long) is no more than the law saith, but it doth not appear vpon the same conueiance or act, that this limitation is nugatorie, but it is forreine matter in respect of the truth of the state whence the lease is deriued: and therefore if lessee for life make a feoffement in fee, yet the state of the lease for yeares is not enlarged against the feoffee, otherwise had it beene if such limitation had not beene but that it had beene left onely to the law. 16.H.7.4. per Keble. 24.Ed.3.28. Fitz.pl.98.

So if tenant after possibility make a lease for yeares, and the donor confirmes to the lessee to hold without impeachment of waste during the life of tenant intaile, this is no more than the law saith, but the priuiledge of tenaunt after possibilitie is forreine matter, as to the lease and confirmation: and therefore if tenant after possibilitie doe surrender, yet the lessee shall hold dispunishab e of waste; otherwise had it been it no such confirmation at all had beene made.

Also heede must be giuen that it be indeed the same thing which the law intendeth, and which the

the partie expresseth, and not like or resembling, and such as may stand both together: for if I let land for life rendring a rent, and by my deede warrant the same land, this warranty in law and warrantie in deed are not the same thing, but may both stand together.

16.Ed.2.Fitz.7 21.Ed.1.zouch. 289.

There remaneth yet a great question on this rule.

A principall reason wherupon this rule is built, should seeme to bee because such acts or clauses are thought to be but declaratorie & added vpon ignorance and *ex consuitudine Clericorum* vpon obseruing of a common forme, and not vpon purpose or meaning, and therefore whether by particular and precise words a man may not controule the intendment of the law.

To this I answer, that no precise or expresse words will controule this intendment of law; but as the generall words are void, because they say contrary to that the law saith; so are they which are thought to bee against the law: and therefore if I demise my land beeing knights seruice tenure to my heire, and expresse my intention to be, that the one part should descend to him as the third appointed by statute, and the other he shall take by deuise to his owne vse, yet this is void; for the law saith hee is in by discent of the whole, and I say, he shall be in by deuise, which

which is against the Law.

But if I make a gift intaile, and say vpon condition, that if tenant intaile discontinue and after die without issue it shall bee lawfull for me to enter; this is a good clause to make a condition, because it is but in one case, and doth not crosse the law generally: for if the tenant intaile in that case bee disseised and a descent cast, and dye without issue, I that am the donor shall not enter. Lit.pl.362.

But if the clause had beene prouided, that if tenant intaile discontinue, or suffer a descent, or doe anie other fact whatsoeuer, that after his death without issue it shall bee lawfull for mee to enter: now this is a voyd condition, for it importeth a repugnancy to law: as if I would ouerrule that where the law saith I am put to my action, I neuerthelesse will reserue to my selfe an entrie.

Non videtur consensum retinuisse si quis ex præscripto minantis aliquid immutauit. Regula 22.

ALthough choise and election bee a badge of consent, yet if the first ground of the act bee duresse, the law will not construe that the duresse doth determine, if the party duressed doe make any motion or offer.

Therefore if a party menace mee, except I make vnto him a bond of 40.l.and I tell him that I will not do it, but I will make vnto him a bond of 20.l. the law ſhall not expound this bond to be voluntarie, but ſhall rather make conſtruction that my minde and courage is not to enter into the greater bond for any menace, and yet that I enter by compulſion,notwithſtanding, into the leſſer.

But if I will draw any conſideration to my ſelfe, as if I had ſaid, I will enter into your bond of 40.l.if you will deliuer me that piece of Plate, now the dureſſe is diſcharged, and yet if it had beene moued from the dureſſor, who had ſaid at the firſt, you ſhall take this piece of Plate, and make me a bond of 40.l.now the gift of the Plate had beene good,and yet the bond ſhall bee auoided by dureſſe.

Regula 23. *Ambiguitas verborum Latens verificatione ſuppletur, nam quod ex facto oritur ambiguum verificatione facti tollitur.*

THere bee two ſorts of ambiguities of words, the one is *Ambiguitas Patens*, and the other *Latens*. *Patens* is that which appeares to bee ambiguous vpon the deed or inſtrument, *Latens* is that which ſeemeth certaine and without ambiguitie, for any thing that appeareth vpon the deed

deed or instrument; but there is some collaterall matter out of the deed, that breedeth the ambiguity.

Ambiguitas Patens is neuer holpen by auerrement, and the reason is, because the law will not couple and mingle matter of specialty, which is of the higher account, with matter of auerrement, which is of inferiour account in law; for that were to make all deedes hollow, and subiect to auerrements, and so in effect, that to passe without deede, which the law appointeth shall not passe but by deed.

Therefore if a man giue land to *I. D. & I. S. & hæredibus*, and doe not limit to whether of their heires, it shall not bee supplied by auerrement to whether of them, the intention was, the inheritance should bee limitted.

So if a man giue land intaile, though it bee by will, the remainder intaile, and adde a *Prouiso*, in this manner: Prouided that if hee or they or any of them doe any &c. according to the vsuall clauses of perpetuities, it cannot be auerred vpon the ambiguities of the reference of this clause, that the intent of the deuisor was, that the restraint should goe onely to him in the remainder, and the heires of his body; and that the tenant intaile in possession, was meant to bee at large.

Of these, infinite cases might be put, for it holdeth generally that all ambiguitie of words by matter within the deed, and not out of the deed, shall bee holpen by construction, or in some case by election, but neuer by auerrement, but rather shall make the deed voide for vncertainty.

But if it be *Ambiguitas latens*, then otherwise it is: as if I graunt my mannour of S. to I. F. and his heires, here appeareth no ambiguitie at all; but if the truth be that I haue the mannours both of South S. and North S. this ambiguity is matter in fact, and therefore it shall bee holpen by auerrement, whether of them was that the party intended should passe.

So if I set forth my land by quantity, then it shall bee supplied by election, and not auerment.

As if I graunt ten acres of wood in sale, where I haue an hundred acres, whether I say it in my deed or no that I graunt out of my hundred acres, yet here shall be an election in the grauntee, which ten hee will take.

And the reason is plaine, for the presumption of the law is, where the thing is onely nominated by quantity, that the parties had indifferent intentions, which should be taken, and there being no cause to helpe the vncertainty by intention, it shall bee holpen by election.

But

But in the former caſe the difference holdeth, where it is expreſſed and where not; for if I recite, Whereas I am ſeiſed of the mannour of North S. and South S. I leaſe vnto you *vnum manerium de S.* there it is clearely an election: ſo if I recite, Where I haue two tenements in St. *Dunſtans*, I leaſe vnto you *vnum tenementum*, there it is an election, not auerment of intention, except the intent were of an election, which may be ſpecially auerred.

Another ſort of *Ambiguitas latens* is correlatiue vnto theſe: for this ambiguitie ſpoken of before, is when one name and appellation doth denominate diuers things, and the ſecond, when the ſame thing is called by diuers names.

As if I giue lands to Chriſt Church in Oxford, and the name of the Corporation is *Eccleſia Chriſti in Vniuerſitate Oxford*, this ſhall be holpen by auerrement, becauſe there appeares no ambiguitie in the words: for this variance is matter in fact, but the auerment ſhall not bee of intention, becauſe it doth ſtand with the words.

For in the caſe of equiuocation the generall intent includes both the ſpeciall, and therefore ſtands with the words: but ſo it is not in variance, and therefore the auerrement muſt be of matter, that doe endure quantitie, and not intention.

As to ſay of the precinct of Oxford, and of the vniuerſitie of Oxeford is one and the ſame, and not to ſay that the intention of the parties was, that the graunt ſhould bee to Chriſt-Church, in that Vniuerſitie of Oxeford.

Regula 24. *Licita bene miſcentur, formula niſi iuris obſtet.*

THe law giueth that fauour to lawfull acts, that although they bee executed by ſeuerall authorities, yet the whole act is good.

As when tenant for life is the remainder in fee, and they ioine in a liuerie by deede or without, this is one good entire liuerie drawne from them both, and doth not inure to a ſurrender of the particular eſtate if it be without deede or confirmation of thoſe in the remainder, if it bee by deede, but they are all parties to the liuery.

Semble cleerement le ley d'eſtre contrary in ambideux caſes, car lou eſt ſans fait eſt liuery ſolement de ceſtui in le rem' & ſurr' de partic' ten' autermen ſera forfeiture de ſon eſtate, & lou eſt per fait le liuerie paſſa ſolement de tenant, car il ad le franktenement, vide accordant. Snr' Co.lib.1.76.b.77.a.Com.Plow.59.A.140. 2.H.5.7.13.H.7.14.13.E.4. 4.a.27.H.8.13.M.16.& 17.El.Dy.339.

So if tenant for life the remainder in fee bee, and they ioine in graunting a rent, this is one ſolid rent out of both their eſtates, and no double rent, or rent by confirmation.

So if tenant intaile be at this day, and he make aleaſe

a leaſe for three liues, and his owne, this is a good leaſe and warranted by the ſtatute of 32. H. 8. and yet it is good in part by the authoritie which tenant intaile hath by the common law, that is, for his own life, and in part by the authoritie which he hath by the ſtatute, that is, for the other three liues. Quære.

So if a man ſeiſed of lands deuiſeable by cuſtome, and of other land held in knights ſeruice, and deuiſe all his lands, this is a good deuiſe of all the land cuſtomarie by the common law, and of two paarts of the other land by the ſtatutes.

So in the Starchamber a ſentence may bee good, grounded in part vpon the authority to giuen the Court by the ſtatute of 3. H. 7. and in part vpon that ancient authoritie which the Court hath by the common law, and ſo vpon ſeuerall commiſſions.

But if there be any forme which law appointeth to bee obſerued, which cannot agree with the diuerſities of authorities, then this rule faileth.

As if three Coparceners be, and one of them alien her purpartie, the feoffee and one of the ſiſters cannot ioine in a writ *de part' facienda*, because it behooueth the feoffee to mention the ſtatute in his writ. Vide 1. Inſtit. 166. b.

Præſentia

Regula 25. *Præsentia corporis tollit errorem Nominis, & veritas nominis tollit errorem Demonstrationis.*

THere be three degrees of certaintie.
1. Presence.
2. Name.
3. Demonstration or Reference.
Whereof the Presence the law holdeth of greatest dignitie, the Name in the second degree, and the Demonstration or Reference in the lowest, and alwayes the errour or falsitie in the lesse worthy.

And therefore if I giue a horse to I.D. being present, and say vnto him, I. S. take this, this is a good gift, notwithstanding I call him by a wrong name; but so had it not beene if I had deliuered him to a stranger to the vse of I.S. where I meant I. D.

So if I say vnto I.S. here I giue you my ring with the Ruby, and deliuer it with my hand, and the Ring beare a Diamond and no Rubie, this is a good gift notwithstanding I name it amisse.

So had it beene if by word or writing without the deliuerie of the thing it selfe, I had giuen the Ring with the Ruby, although I had no such, but only one with a Diamond which I meant, yet it would haue passed.

So

So if I by deede graunt vnto you by generall words, all the lands that the King hath passed vnto me by letters pattents dated 10. May vnto this present Indenture annexed, and the Pattent annexed haue date 10. Iuly, yet if it bee proued that that was the true Pattent annexed, the presence of the Pattent maketh the error of the date recited not materiall; yet if no Pattent had been annexed, and there had beene also no other certaintie giuen, but the reference of the Pattent, the date whereof was mis-recited, although I had no other Pattent euer of the King, yet nothing would haue passed.

Like law is it, but more doubtfull, where there is not a presence but a kinde of representation, which is lesse worthie than a presence, and yet more worthie than a Name or Reference.

As if I couenant with my Ward, that I will tender vnto him no other marriage, than the gentlewoman, whose picture I deliuered him, and that picture hath about it *Ætatis suæ anno.* 16. and the gentlewoman is seuenteene yeares old, yet neuerthelesse if it can bee proued that the picture was made for that gentlewoman, I may notwithstanding this mistaking, tender her well enough.

So if I graunt you for life a way ouer my land according to a plot intended betweene vs, and after

after I graunt vnto you and your heires a way according to the first plot intended, whereof a table is annexed to these presents, and there bee some speciall variance betweene the table and the originall plot, yet this representation shall be certaintie sufficient to lead vnto the first plot, and you shall haue the way in fee neuerthelesse, according to the first plot, and not according to the table.

So if I graunt vnto you by generall words the land which the King hath graunted mee by his letters pattents, *Quarum tenor sequitur in hæc verba,&c.* and there bee some mistaking in the recitall and variance from the originall pattent, although it bee in a point materiall, yet the representation of this whole pattent shall bee as the annexing of the true pattent, and the graunt shall not be void by this variance.

Now for the second part of this rule touching the Name and the Reference, for the explaining thereof, it must bee noted what things sound in demonstration or addition: as first in lands, the greatest certaintie is, where the land hath a name proper, as the mannor of Dale, Grandfield, &c. the next is equall to that, when the land is set forth by bounds and abuttals, as a close of pasture bounding on the East part vpon Emsdenwood, on the South vpon, &c. It is also a sufficient name to lay the generall boundarie, that is, some

ſome place of larger precinct, if there be no other land to paſſe in the ſame precinct, as all my lands in Dale, my tenement in S. Dunſtans pariſh, &c.

A farther ſort of denomination is to name land by the attendancy they haue to other lands more notorious, as parcell of my manour of D. belonging to ſuch a Colledge lying vpon Thames banke.

All theſe things are notes found in denomination of lands, becauſe they be ſignes to call, and therefore of propertie to ſignifie and name a place; but theſe notes that ſound only in demonſtration and addition, are ſuch as are but tranſitorie and accidentall to the nature of the place.

As *modo in tenura & occupatione,* of the proprietorie tenure or poſſeſſor is but a thing tranſitorie in reſpect of land; *Generatio venit, generatio migrat, terra autem manet in æternum.*

So likewiſe matter of conueiance, title, or inſtrument,

As, *quæ perquiſiui de I.D. quæ deſcendebant à I.N. patre meo,* or, *in prædicta Indentura dimiſsionis,* or, *in prædictis literis patentibus ſpecificat.*

So likewiſe *continent' per æſtimationem* 20. *acras,* or if *(per æſtimationem)* be left out, all is one, for

For it is vnderſtood, and this matter of meaſure, although it ſeeme locall, yet it is indeede but opinion and obſeruation of men.

The diſtinction beeing made, the rule is to bee examined by it.

Therefore if I graunt my cloſe called Dale in in the pariſh of Hurſt, in the Countie of Southhampton, and the pariſh likewiſe extendeth into the Countie of Barkſhire, and the whole cloſe of Dale lieth in the Countie of Barkſhire, yet becauſe the parcell is eſpecially named, the falſitie of the addition hurteth not, and yet this addition is found in name, but (as it was ſaid) it was leſſe worthie than a proper name.

So if I graunt *tenementum meum*, or *omnia tenementa mea* (for the vniuerſall and indefinite to this purpoſe are all one) *in parochia Sancti Butolphi extra Aldgate* (where the veritie is *extra Biſhopſgate) in tenura Guilielmi*, which is true, yet this grant is void, becauſe that which ſounds in denomination is falſe which is the more worthy, and that which ſounds in addition is true which is the leſſe; * and though *in tenura Guili lmi*, which is true had beene firſt placed, yet it had beene all one.

* Semble icy le grant vſt eſte aſſets bon, cõe fuit reſolu per Cur', Co lib. 3. fo. 10. a. vide 33 H. 8. Dy. 50. b. 12. Eliz. ib. 292. b. & Co. lib. 2. fo. 33. a.

Vide ib. quæ contraria eſt lex, car icy auxi le primer certainty eſt faux.

But if I graunt *tenementum meum quod perquiſiui de R.C. in Dale*, where the truth was T.C. and

I haue

I haue no other tenements in D. but one, this graunt is good, becaufe that which foundeth in name (*viz.* in Dale) is true, and that which founded in addition (*viz. quod perquisiui, &c.*) is onely falfe.

So if I graunt *Prata mea in Sale continentia* 10. *acras*, and they containe indeede 20 acres, the whole 20. paffe.

So if I graunt all my lands, being parcels *manerij de D. in prædictis literis patentibus fpecificat'*, and there bee no letters pattents, yet the graunt is good enough.

The like reafon holds in demonftrations of perfons that haue beene declared in demonftration of lands and places, the proper name of euerie one is in certaintie worthieft, next are fuch appellations as are fixed to his perfon, or at leaft of continuance, as fonne of fuch a man, wife of fuch a husband; or addition of office, as Clerke of fuch a Court, &c. and the third are actions or accidents, which found no way in appellation or name, but onely in circumftance, which are leffe worthie, although they may haue a poore particular reference to the intention of the graunt.

And therefore if an obligation be made to I.S. *filio & hæredi G.S.* where indeede he is a baftard, yet this obligation is good.

So if I grant land *Episcopo nunc Londinensi qui me erudiuit in pueritia*, this is a good graunt, although he neuer instructed me.

But *è conuersò*, if I grant land to I. S. *filio & hæredi G.S.* and it bee true that hee is sonne and heire vnto G.S. but his name is Thomas, this is a void grant.

Or if in the former graunt it was the Bishop of Canterburie who taught mee in my childhood, yet shall it be good (as was said) to the Bishop of London, and not to the Bishop of Canterburie.

The same rule holdeth of denomination of times, which are such a day of the Moneth, such a day of the weeke, such a Saints day or Eaue, To day, to morrow; these are names of times.

But the day that I was borne, the day that I was married; these are but circumstances and addition of times.

And therefore if I binde my selfe to doe some personall attendance vpon you vpon Innocents day being the day of your birth, and you were not borne that day, yet shall I attend.

There resteth two questions of difficultie yet vpon this rule: first, of such things whereof men take not so much note as that they shall faile of this

this distinction of name and addition.

As my boxe of Iuorie lying in my study sealed vp with my seale of armes, my suite of Arras with the storie of the Natiuitie and Passion; of such things there can be no name, but all is of description, and of circumstance, and of these I hold the law to bee, that precise truth of all recited circumstances is not required.

But in such things *ex multitudine signorum colligitur identitas vera,* therefore though my boxe were sealed, and although the arras had the storie of the natiuitie and not of the passion, if I had no other boxe nor no other suite, the gifts are good, and there is certaintie sufficient, for the law doth not expect a precise description of such things as haue no certaine denomination.

Secondly of such things as doe admit the distinction of name and addition, but the notes fall out to bee of equall dignitie all of name or addition.

As, *prata mea iuxta communem fossam in D.* whereof the one is true, the other false, or, *tenementum meum in tenura Guilielmi quod perquisiui de R.C. in predict' Indent' specificat'* whereof one is true and two are false, or two are true and one false.

So *ad curiam quam tenebat die mercurii tertio die*

die Martii, wherof the one is true the other falſe.

In theſe caſes the former rule *ex multitudine ſignorum,&c.* holdeth not, neither is the placing of the falſitie or veritie firſt or laſt materiall, but all muſt be true, or elſe the graunt is void, alwaies vnderſtood, that if you can reconcile all the words, and make no falſitie, that is quiteout of this rule, which hath place onely where there is a direct contrarietie, or falſity not to be reconciled to this rule.

Vide liuers auantdit pur ceſt auxi.

As if I graunt all my land in D. *in tenura I.S.* which I purchaſed of I.N. ſpecified in a deuiſe to I.D. and I haue land in D. whereof in part of them all theſe circumſtances are true, but I haue other lands in D. wherein ſome of them faile, this graunt will not paſſe all my land in D. for there theſe are references and no words of falſitie or error but of limitation and reſtraint.

FINIS.

THE USE OF THE LAVV.

Provided for Preſervation OF

Our { *Perſons*, *Goods*, and *Good Names*. }

According to the Practiſe OF

The { *Lawes and Cuſtomes* } *of this Land.*

By the L: Verulam Viſcount of S. *Albons* &c.

LONDON,
Printed by the Aſſignes of IOHN MOORE Eſquire. 1630.

A Table of the Contents of this ensuing Treatise.

 was

Recogni-

THE TABLE.

 Land

THE TABLE.

Hee

9. By

THE

THE VSE OF THE LAVV,

And wherein it Principally Consisteth.

THE Vse of the Law, consisteth principally in these Three things:

1 To secure Mens persons from Death and Violence.
2 To dispose the propertie of their Goods and Lands.
3 For preseruation of their good Names from shame and Infamie.

FOr safetie of persons, the Law prouideth, that any man standing in feare of another, may (Surety to keepe the Peace.)

may take his Oath before a Iustice of Peace, that hee ſtandeth in feare of his life, and the Iustice ſhall compell the other to be bound with Suerties to keepe the Peace.

Action of the Caſe, for Slaunder, Batterie, &c.

If any man Beate, wound or maime another, or giue falſe ſcandalous words that may touch his Credit, the Law giueth thereupon an action of the Caſe, for the ſlaunder of his good name; and an Action of Batterie, or an appeale of Maime, by which recompence ſhall be recouered, to the value of the hurt, damage or danger.

Appeale of Murther giuen to the next of kinne.

If any man kill another with malice, the Law giueth an appeale to the wife of the dead, if hee had any, or to the next of kinne that is Heire in default of a Wife, by which appeale the Defendant conuicted is to ſuffer Death, and to loſe all his Lands and Goods; But if the Wife or Heire will not ſue or bee compounded withall, yet the King is to puniſh the offence by Indictment or Preſentment of a lawfull inqueſt & tryall of the Offenders before competent Iudges; whereupon being found guiltie, hee is to ſuffer Death, and to loſe his lands and goods.

Man ſlaughter, and when a forfeiture of Goods, and when not.

If one kill another vpon a ſuddain quarrell, this is Man-ſlaughter, for which the Offender muſt dye, except he can reade; and if hee can

can reade, yet must hee lose his goods, but no lands.

And if a man kill another in his owne defence, hee shall not lose his Life, nor his Lands, but he must lose his Goods, except the partie slaine did first assault him, to kill, robbe, or trouble him by the High-way side, or in his owne House, and then he shall lose nothing.

And if a man kill himselfe, all his Goods and Chattels are forfeited, but no Lands. Felon: de Se.

If a man kill another by misfortune, as shooting an Arrow at a Butt or Marke, or casting a Stone ouer an house, or the like, this is losse of his goods and Chattels, but not of his lands, nor life. Felony by mischance.

If a Horse, or Cart, or a Beast, or any other thing doe kill a man, the Horse, Beast or other thing is forfeited to the Crowne, & is called a *Deodand*, and vsually graunted and allowed by the King to the Bishop Almner, as goods are of those that kill themselues. Deodand.

The Cutting out of a mans Tongue, or putting out his Eyes maliciously, is Felonie; for which the offender is to suffer Death, and lose his lands and goods. Cutting out of Tongues and putting out of Eyes, made Felonie.

But, for that all Punishment is for Examples sake; it is good to see the meanes whereby Offenders are drawne to their punishment; and first for matter of the peace.

THe auncient Lawes of England planted heere by the Conquerour, were, that there should be Officers of two sorts in all the parts of this Realme to preserue the Peace:

1. *Constabularij* } *Pacis.*
2. *Conseruatores* }

The Office of the Constable:

The Office of the Constable was, to arrest the parties that hee had seene breaking the Peace, or in furie ready to breake the peace, or was truely informed by others, or by their owne confession, that they had freshly broken the peace; which persons he might imprison in the Stockes, or in his owne house, as his or their quality required, vntill they had become bounden with sureties to keepe the peace; which obligation from thenceforth, was to be sealed and deliuered to the Constable to the vse of the King. And that the Constable was to send to the Kings Exchequer or Chancery, from whence Processe should bee awarded to leauy the debt, if the peace were broken.

But

But the Conſtable could not arreſt any, nor make any put in Bond vpon complaint of threatning onely, except they had ſeene them breaking the peace, or had come freſhly after the peace was broken. Alſo, theſe Conſtables ſhould keepe watch about the Towne for the apprehenſion of Rogues and Vagabonds, and Night-walkers, & Eueſdroppers, Scouts, and ſuch like, and ſuch as goe Armed. And they ought likewiſe to raiſe hue and cry againſt Murtherers, Manſlayers, Theeues and Rogues.

First, High Conſtables, 2.ly, Pettie Conſtables.

2. High Conſtables for euery hundred.

1. Pettie Conſtable for euery village.

Of this Office of Conſtable there were high Conſtables, two of euery Hundred; Pettie Conſtables one in euery Village, they were in ancient time all appointed by the Sheriffe of the Shiere yearely in his Court called the Sheriffes Tourne, and there they receiued their oath. But at this day they are appointed eyther in the Law day of that Precinct wherin they ſerue, or elſe by the high Conſtable in the Seſſions of the peace.

The Kings Bench firſt inſtituted, and in what matters they anciently had Iuriſdiction.

The Sheriffes Tourne is a Court very ancient, incident to his Office. At the firſt, it was erected by the Conquerour, and called the Kings-Bench, appointing men ſtudied in the Knowledge of the Lawes to execute Iuſtice, as ſubſtitutes to him in his name, which men are to be named, *Iusticiarij ad placita coram Rege assignati*. One of them being *Capitalis Iusticiarius* called to his fellowes, the rest in number as pleaseth the King, of late but three *Iusticiarij*, holden by Patent. In this Court euery man aboue twelue yeares of age, was to take his Oath of Allegeance to the King, if hee were bound, then his Lord to answere for him. In this Court the Constables were appointed and sworne; breakers of the peace punished by fine and imprisonment, the parties beaten or hurt recompenced vpon complaints of damages, All appeales of Murther, Maime, Robberie decided, contempts against the Crowne, publique annoyances against the people, Treasons and Felonies, and all other matters of wrong, betwixt partie and partie for Lands and goods.

Court of Marshalsee erected, and its Iurisdiction within 12. miles of the chiefe Tunnel of the King, which is the full extent of the Virge.

But the King seeing the Realme grow daily more and more populous, and that this one Court could not dispatch all, did first ordain that his Marshall should keepe a Court, for Controuersies arising within the *Virge*. Which is within xii. miles of the chiefest Tunnell of the Court, which did but ease the Kings Bench in matters onely concerning debts, Couenants, and such like, of those of the Kings houshold onely, neuer dealing in breaches of the Peace, or concerning the Crowne

Crowne by any other perſons, or any pleas of Lands. Inſomuch, as the King for further eaſe hauing diuided this Kingdome into Counties, and committing the Charge of euery Countie to a Lord or Earle; did direct, that thoſe Earles within their limits ſhould looke to the matter of the peace, and take charge of the Conſtables, and reforme publike annoyances, and ſweare the people to the Crowne, & take pledges of the Freemen for their Allegeance, for which purpoſe the Countie did once euery yeare keep a Court, called the Sheriffes Tourne. At which all the Countie (except Women, Clergie, Children vnder 12. and not aged aboue 60.) did appeare to giue or renew their pledges for Allegeance. And the Court was called, *Curia Franci plegij*, A view of the pledges of Free-men; or, *Turnus Comitatus*.

Sheriffes Tourne inſtituted vpon the diuiſion of England into Counties, the charge of this Court was committed to the Earle of the ſame Countie: this was likewiſe called *Curia Viſus fra. pleg.*

At which meeting or Court, there fell by occaſion of great Aſſemblies much bloudſhed, ſcarcitie of Victuals, Mutinies, and the like miſchiefes; which are incident to the Congregations of people, by which the King was moued to allow a ſubdiuiſion of euery Countie into Hundreds, and euery Hundred to haue a Court, whereunto the people of euery Hundred ſhould be aſſembled twice a yeare for ſurueigh of Pledges, and vſe of that Iuſtice which was formerly executed in that grand

Subdiuiſion of the Countie Court into Hundreds.

grand Court for the Countie; and the Count or Earle appointed a Bayliffe vnder him to keepe the hundred Court. But in the end, the Kings of this Realme found it necessarie to haue all execution of Iustice immediately from themselues, by such as were more bound then Earles to that seruice, and readily subiect to correction for their negligence or abuse; and therefore, tooke to themselues the appointing of a Sheriffe yearely in euery Countie, calling them *Vicecomites*, and to them directed such writs and precepts for executing Iustice in the Countie, as fell out needfull to haue beene dispatched, committing to the Sheriffe *Custodium Comitatus*; by which the Earles were spared of their toyles and labours, and that was layd vpon the Sheriffes. So as now, the Sheriffe doth all the Kings businesse in the Countie, and that is now called, the Sheriffes Tourne; that is to say, he is Iudge of this grand Court for the Countie, and also of all Hundred Courts not giuen away from the Crowne.

The charge of the Countie taken from the Earles, and committed yearely to such persons as it pleased the King.

The Sheriffe is Iudge of all Hundred Courts not giuen away from the Crowne.

County Court kept monethly by the Sheriffe.

Hee hath another Court, called the Countie Court, belonging to his office, wherein men may sue monethly for any debt or damages vnder 40[s]. and may haue writs for to repleuie their cattell distrained and impounded by others, and there try the cause of their distresse; and by a writ called *Iusticies*, a man a man may ſue for any ſumme, and in this Court the Sheriffe by a writ, called an Exigent, doth proclaime men ſued in Courts aboue, to render their bodies, or elſe they be Out-lawed.

This Sheriffe doth ſerue the Kings writs of Proceſſe, be they Sommons, Attachments to compell men to anſwer to the Law, and all writs of execution of the Law, according to Iudgements of Superiour Court, for taking of Mens Goods, Lands, or Bodies, as the cauſe requireth.

The Office of the Sheriffe.

The Hundred Courts, were moſt of them granted to Religious Men, Noble men, and others of great place. And alſo many men of good quality haue attained by Charter, and ſome by vſage within Mannors of their owne liberty of keeping Law dayes, and to vſe there Iuſtice appertaining to a Law day.

Hundred Courts to whom they were at firſt granted.

Whoſoeuer is Lord of the Hundred Court, is to appoint two high Conſtables of the Hundred, and alſo is to appoint in euery Village, a pettie Conſtable with a Tithingman to attend in his abſence, and to be at his Commandement when hee is preſent in all ſeruices of his office for his aſſiſtance.

Lord of the Hundred to appoint two High Conſtables.

There hath beene by vſe and Statute Law

(besides furueying of the Pledges of Free-men,and giuing the oath of Allegeance, and making Conftables,) many additions of powers and authority giuen to the Stewards of Leets and Lawdayes to be put in vre in their Courts; as for example, they may punifh Inne-keepers,Victuallers,Bakers,Butchers,Poulterers, Fifhmongers, and Tradefmen of all forts, felling with vnder weights or meafures or at exceffiue prizes, or things vnwholfome, or ill made in deceipt of the people.They may punifh thofe that do ftop, ftraiten or annoy the high wayes, or doe not according to the prouifion enacted,repaire or amend them,or diuert water courfes, or deftroy frey of Fifh, or vfe engines or nets to take Deere, Conies, Phefants or Partridges, or build Pigeon houfes;except he be Lord of the Mannor,or Parfon of the Church. They may alfo take prefentment vpon Oath of the xii.fworne Iury before them of all felonies; but they cannot try the Malefactors, onely they muft by Indenture deliuer ouer thofe prefentments of felonie to the Iudges,when they come their circuits into that Countie. All thofe Courts before mentioned are in vfe,and exercifed as Law at this day,concerning the Sheriffes Law dayes and Leets, and the offices of High Conftables, pettie-Conftables,and Tithingmen; howbeit,with fome further additions by Statute lawes, laying

Of what matters they enquire of in Leets and Law dayes.

charge

charge vpon them for taxation for poore, for Souldiers, and the like, and dealing without corruption, and the like.

Conseruators of the Peace were in ancient times certaine, which were assigned by the King to see the Peace maintained, and they were called to the Office by the Kings writ, to continue for terme of their liues, or at the Kings pleasure.

Conseruators of the Peace called by the Kings writ for terme of their liues, or at the Kings pleasure.

For this Seruice, choise was made of the best men of calling in the Countrie, and but few in the Shire. They might bind any man to keepe the peace and to good behauiour, by Recognizance to the King with suerties, and they might by Warrant send for the partie, directing their warrant to the Sheriffe or Constable, as they please, to arrest the partie, and bring him before them. This they vsed to doe, when complaint was made by any that he stood in feare of another, & so tooke his Oath; or else, where the Conseruator himselfe did without oath or complaint, see the disposition of any man inclined to quarrell and breach of the Peace, or to misbehaue himselfe in some outragious manner of force or fraud, There by his owne Discretion he might send for such a fellow, and make him finde Suerties of the peace or of his good behauiour, as he should see cause; or

Conseruators of the Peace, and what their Office was.

else commit him to the Goale if he refused.

Conseruators of the Peace by vertue of their Office.

The Iudges of either Bench in *Westminster*, Barons of the Exchequer, Master of the Rolles, and Iustices in Eire and Assizes in their circuits, were all without writ Conseruators of the Peace in all Shires of England, and continue to this day.

Iustices of Peace ordained in lieu of Conseruators. Power of placing and displacing Iustic. of Peace by vse deligated from the King to the Chanchellor.

But now at this day, Conseruators of the Peace are out of vse; And in lieu of them, there are ordained Iustices of Peace, assigned by the Kings Commissions in euery Countie, which are moueable at the Kings pleasure; but the power of placing and displacing Iustices of the Peace, is by vse Deligated from the King to the Chancellor.

That there should be Iustices of Peace by Commissions, it was first enacted by a Statute made 1. *Edw*.3. and their Authoritie augmented by many statutes made since in euery Kings reigne.

a The power of the Iust. of Peace, to fine the Offenders to the Crowne, and not to recompence the partie grieued. Parle Statut. 17 R. 2. Cap. 10. & v. *Dier*. 69: b. Ils eunt poiar d'inquier de murder car. ce Felon.

a They are appointed to keepe foure Sessions euery yeare; That is, euery Quarter one. These Sessions are a sitting of the Iustices to dispatch the affaires of their Commissions. They haue power to heare and determine in their Sessions, all Felonies, breaches of the Peace, Contempts and trespasses, so farre as to fine the Offender to the Crowne, but not

to

to award recompence to the partie grieued.

They are to suppresse Ryots, and Tumults, to restore Possessions forcibly taken away, to examine all Felons apprehended & brought before them; To see impotent poore people, or maimed Souldiers prouided for, according to the Lawes. And Rogues, Vagabonds, and Beggers punished. They are both to Licence and suppresse Alehouses, Badgers of Corne and Victuals, and to punish Forestallers, regrators, and engrossers.

Authority of the Iustices of Peace, through whom run all the Countie seruices vnto the Crowne.

Through these in effect runne all the Countie seruices to the Crowne, as Taxations of Subsidies, Mustring men, Arming them, and leauying Forces, that is done by a speciall Commission or Precept from the King. Any of these Iustices by Oath taken by a man that hee standeth in feare that another man will beate him, or kill him, or burne his House, are to send for the partie by warrant of Attachment directed to the Sheriffe or Constable, and then to bind the party with Suerties by Recognizance to the King to keepe the peace, and also to appeare at the next Sessions of the Peace; at which next Sessions, when euery Iustice of Peace hath therein deliuered all their Recognizances so taken, then the parties are called and the cause of binding to the Peace examined, and both parties being heard, the whole Bench is

Beating, killing, burning of Houses. Attachments for suretie of the Peace.

Recognizance of the Peace deliuered by the Iustices at their Sessions.

to determine as they see cause, either to continue the partie so bound, or else to discharge him.

Quarter Sessions held by the Iustices of the Peace.

The Iustices of Peace in their Sessions, are attended by the Constables and Bayliffes of all Hundreds and liberties within the Countie, and by the Sheriffe or his Deputy, to bee employed as occasion shal serue in executing the precepts and directions of the Court. They proceed in this sort, The Sheriffe doth Summon 24. Free-holders, discreet men of the said County, wherof some 16. are selected and sworne, and haue their charge to serue as the Grand Iury; The partie indicted is to trauerse the indictment, or else to confesse it, and so submit himselfe to bee fined as the Court shall thinke meet (regard had to the offence) except the punishment be certainly appointed (as often it is) by speciall Statutes.

The Iustices of Peace are many in euerie Countie, & to them are brought all Traitors, Felons, and other malefactors of any sort vpon their first apprehension, and that Iustice to whom they are brought, examineth them, and heareth their accusations, but iudgeth not vpon it; onely if hee find the suspicion but light, then hee taketh bond with sureties of the accused, to appeare either at the next Assizes, if it be a matter of Treason or Felonie;

nie; or else at the quarter Sessions, if it bee concerning Ryot or mis-behauior, or some other small offence. And he also then bindeth to appeare those that giue testimonie and prosecute the accusation, all the accusers and witnesses, and so setteth the partie at large. And at the Assizes or Sessions (as the case falleth out) he certifieth the Recognizances taken of the Accused, Accusers, and Witnesses, who being there are called, and appearing, the cause of the accused is debt, according to Law for his clearing or condemning.

The authority of Iustices of the Peace out of their Sessions.

But if the partie accused, seeme vpon pregnant matter in the accusation and to the Iustice to bee guilty, and the offence heinous, or the Offender taken with the manner, then the Iustice is to commit the partie by his warrant called a *Mittimus* to the Goaler of the common Goale of the Countie, there to remaine vntill the Assizes. And then the Iustice is to certifie his Accusation, Examination, and Recognizance taken for the appearances and prosecution of the witnesses, so as the Iudges may, when they come, readily proceed with him as the Law requireth.

The Iudges of the Assizes as they bee now become into the place of the ancient Iustices in Eyre, called *Iusticiarij itinerantes*, which in the prime Kings after the Conquest vntill

Iudges of Assize come in place of the ancient Iudges in Eyre about the time of R. 2.

H. 3.

H.3. time especially, and after in lesser measure euen to *R*.2.time,did execute the Iustice of the Realme; they began in this sort.

1.Kings Bench
2.Marshals Court.
3.Countie Court.
4. Sheriffes Tournes.
5. Hundred Leets & Law-dayes. All which dealt only in Crown matters,butthe Iustice in Eyre dealt in priuate titles of lands or goods,and in all Treasons and Felonies, of whom there were 12. in number, the whole Realme being diuided into six Circuits.

England diuided into six Circuits,& two learned men in the Lawes, assigned by the Kings Commission to ride twice a yeare through those Shires allotted to that Circuit,for their tryall of priuate titles to lands and goods, and all Treasons and Felonies, which the Countie Courts meddle not in.

The authoritie, of Tourns,Leets, Hundreds, and Law-dayes, as it was confirmed to some speciall causes touching the publike good.

The King not able to dispatch busines in his owne person, erected the Court of Kings Bench, that not able to receiue all, nor meet to draw the people all to one place, there were ordained Counties, and the Sheriffes Tournes, Hundred Courts, and particular Leets, and Law-dayes,as before mentioned, which dealt onely with Crowne matters for the publique; but not the priuate titles of Lands or Goods,nor the tryall of grand offences of Treasons and Felonies, but all the Counties of the Realme were diuided into Six Circuites. And two learned men well read in the Lawes of the Realme, were assigned by the Kings Commission to euery Circuit, and to ride twice a yeare through those shires allotted to that Circuit, making Proclamation before hand, a conuenient time in euery Countie, of the time of their comming,and place of their sitting,to the end the people might attend them in euery Countie of that Circuit.

They

They were to stay 3. or 4. dayes in euery Countie, and in that time all the causes of that Countie were brought before them by the parties grieued, and all the Prisoners of the said Goale in euery Shire, and whatsoeuer controuersies arising concerning Life, Lands or Goods.

The authoritie of these Iudges in Eyre, is in part translated by Act of Parliament to Iustices of Assize; which be now the Iudges of Circuits, and they doe vse the same Course that Iustices in Eyre did, to proclaime their comming euery halfe yeare, and the place of their sitting.

The authority translated by Parliament to Iustices of Assize.

The businesse of the Iustices in Eyre, and of the Iustices of Assize at this day is much lessened, for that in *H.*3. time there was erected the Court of Common-pleas at Westminster, In which Court haue beene euer since and yet are, begun and handled the great suits of Lands, debts, benefices and contracts, fines for assurance of Lands and recoueries, which were wont to bee either in the Kings Bench, or else before the Iustices in Eyre. But the Statute of *Mag. Char. Cap.* 11. 5. is negatiue against it. *Viz. Communia placita non sequantur, Curiam nostram sed teneantur in aliquo loco Certo*; which *locus Certus* must be the Common-pleas; yet the Iudges of Circuits

The authoirty of the Iustices of Assizes much lessened by the Court of Common Pleas, erected in H. 3. time.

The Iustices of Assize haue at this day 5. Cõmissions by which they sit 1 Oyer and Termin. 2 Goale Deliuery. 3 To take Assizes. 4 To take Nisi Prius. 5 Of the Peace

cuits haue now fiue Commissions by which they sit.

Oyer and Terminer, in which the Iudges are of the Quorum, and this is the largest Commission they haue.

The first is a Commission of Oyer and Terminer, directed vnto them, and many others of the best accompt, in their Circuits; But in this Commission the Iudges of Assize are of the *Quorum*, so as without them there can be no proceeding.

This Commission giueth them power to deale with Treasons, Murthers, and all manner of Felonies and Misdemeanours whatsoeuer; and this is the largest Commission that they haue.

Goale deliuery directed onely to the Iudges themselues, and the Cleark of the Assize.

The second is a Commission of Goale Deliuery; That is only to the Iudges themselues, & the Clearke of the Assize associate: And by this Commission they are to deale with euery Prisoner in the Goale, for what offence soeuer he be there And to proceed with him according to the Lawes of the Realme, & the quality of his offence; And they cannot by this Commission doe any thing concerning any man, but those that are Prisoners in the Goale. The course now in vse of Execution of this Commission of Goale Deliuery, is this. There is no Prisoner but is committed by some Iustice of Peace, who

who before he committed him tooke his examination, and bound his accusers and witnesses to appeare and prosecute at the Goale deliuery. This Iustice doth certifie these examinations and bonds, and thereupon the Accuser is called solemnely into the Court; and when he appeareth he is willed to prepare a Bill of indictment against the Prisoner, and goe with it to the grand-Iury, and giue euidence vpon their oathes, he and the witnesses; which he doth: and then the Grand Iury write thereupon either *Billa vera*, & then the Prisoner standeth indicted, or else *Ignoramus*, and then he is not touched. The Grand Iury deliuer these Bils to the Iudges in their Court, and so many as they find indorsed *Billa vera*, they send for those Prisoners, then is euery mans indictment put and read to him, and they aske him whether hee be guilty or not, if he saith guilty, his confession is recorded; if hee say not guilty, then hee is asked how hee will bee tryed; hee answereth, by the Countrey. Then the Sheriffe is commanded to returne the names of 12. Freeholders to the Court, which Freeholders be sworne to make true deliuery betweene the King and the Prisoner, and then the indictment is againe read and the witnesses sworne, to speake their knowledge concerning the fact, and the Prisoner is heard at large, what de-

The manner of the proceedings of the Iustices of Circuits in their Circuits.

The course now in vse with the Iudges for the execution of the Commission of Goale deliuery.

fence

fence hee can make, and then the Iury goe together and consult. And after a while they come in with a verdict of guilty or not guiltie, which verdict the Iudges doe record accordingly. If any Prisoner plead not guilty vpon the indictment, and yet will not put himselfe to tryall vpon the Iury, (or stand mute) he shall be pressed.

The Iudges when many prisoners are in the Goale, doe in the end before they goe, peruse euery one. Those that were indicted by Grand Iury, and found not guiltie by the select Iury, they iudge to be quitted, and so deliuer them out of the Goale. Those that are found guilty by both Iuries they Iudge to death, and command the Sheriffe to see execution done. Those that refuse tryall by the Countrie, or stand mute vpon the indictment, they iudge to be pressed to death, some whose offences are pilfring vnder twelue pence value, they iudge to be whipped. Those that confesse their indictments, they iudge to death, whipping or otherwise, as their offence requireth. And those that are not indicted at all, but their bill of indictment returned with *Ignoramus* by the Grand Iury, and all other in the Goale against whom no bils at all are preferred, they doe acquit by proclamation out of the Goale; That one way or other they ridde the Goale of all the prisoners in it. But because some

prisoners

prisoners haue their bookes, and be burned in the hand and so deliuered, It is necessary to shew the reason thereof. This hauing their bookes is called their Clergie, which in ancient time began thus.

For the scarcity of the Clergie in the Realme of England, to be disposed in Religious houses, or for Priests, Deacons and Clerkes of parishes, there was a prerogatiue allowed to the Clergie, that if any man that could reade as a Clerke, were to be condemned to death, the Bishop of the Diocesse, might if he would, clayme him as a clerke, & he was to see him tryed in the face of the Court.

Booke allowed to Clergie for the scarcitie of them to be disposed in Religious Houses.

Whether he could read or not the booke was prepared and brought by the Bishop, and the Iudge was to turne to some place as he should thinke meete, and if the prisoner could reade, then the Bishop was to haue him deliuered ouer vnto him to dispose of in some places of the Clergie, as hee should thinke meete. But if either the Bishop would not demand him: or that the Prisoner could not read, then was hee to be put to death.

And this Clergie was allowable in the ancient times and Law, for all offences whatsoeuer they were, except Treason and robbing of Churches of their goods and ornaments.

Concerning the allowing of the Clergie to the Prisoner.

Clergy allowed in all offences except Treason and Robbing of Churches, and now taken away by many Statutes.
1. In Treason.
2. In Burglarie.
3. Robberie.
4. Purse-cutting
5. Horse stealing, and in diuers other offences particularized in seuerall Statutes.
By the Stat. of 18. Eliz. the Iudges are appointed to allow Clergie, & to see them burned in the hand, and to discharge the Prisoners without deliuering them to the Bishop.

naments. But by many Statutes made since, the Clergie is taken away for Murther, Burglarie, Robberie, Purse-cutting, horsestealing, and diuers other felonies particularized by the Statutes to the Iudges; and lastly, by a Statute made 18. *Elizabeth*, the Iudges themselues are appointed to allow Clergie to such as can read, being not such offenders from whom Clergie is taken away by any Statute, And to see them burned in the hand, and so discharge them without deliuering them to the Bishop, howbeit the Bishop appointeth the deputy to attend the Iudges with a booke to trie whether they could reade or not.

The third Commission that the Iudges of Circuits haue, is, a Commission directed to themselues onely and the Clerke of Assize to take Assizes, by which they are called Iustices of Assize, & the Office of those Iustices is to doe right vpon Writs called Assizes, brought before them by such as are wrongfully thrust out of their Lands. Of which number of writs there was farre greater store brought before them in ancient times than now, for that mens seizons & possessions are sooner recouered by sealing Leases vpon the ground, and by bringing an *Eiectione firme*, and trying their title so, than by the long suites of Assizes.

The fourth Commission, is a Commission

to

to take *Nisi Prius* directed to none but to the Iudges themselues and their Clerkes of Assizes, by which they are called Iustices of *Nisi Prius*. These *Nisi Prius* happen in this sort, When a suit is begun for any matter in one of the three Courts, the Kings Bench, Common Pleas, or the Exchequer here aboue, and the parties in their pleadings doe varie in a point of fact; As for example, If in an action of Debt vpon obligation the defendant denies the obligation to be his debt, or in any action of trespasse growne for taking away goods, the Defendant denieth that hee tooke them, or in an action of the Case for slaunderous words, the Defendant denieth that hee spake them, &c.

4. Commission is to take Nisi Prius: and this is directed to two Iudges & the Clerke of the Assize.

Nisi Prius.

Then the Plaintiffe is to maintaine and proue that the obligation is the Defendants deed, that he either tooke the goods, or spake the words; vpon which deniall and affirmation the Law saith, that Issue is ioyned betwixt them, which issue of the Fact is to be tried by a Iurie of Twelue men of the Countie where it is supposed by the Plaintiffe to be done, & for that purpose the Iudges of the Court do award a writ of *Venire fac*: in the Kings name to the Sheriffe of that Countie, commanding him to cause foure and twentie descreet Freeholders of his Countie at a certaine day to try this issue so ioyned, out of which foure and twenty, only Twelue are chosen to serue.

Ven. fac. pr. 24.

Free-holders.

And

And that double number is returned, because some may make default, and some bee challenged vpon kindred, alliance, or partiall dealing.

These foure and twentie, the Sheriffe doth name and certifie to the Court, and withall that he hath warned them to come at the day according to their writ. But because at his first summons there falleth no punishment vpon the foure and twentie if they come not, they very seldome or neuer appeare vpon the first Writ, and vpon their default there is another Writ * returned to the Sheriffe, commaunding him to distraine them by their Lands to appeare at a certaine day appointed by the writ, which is the next terme after, *Nisi prius Iusticiarij nostri ad Assizas capiendas Venerint, &c.* of which words the writ is called a *Nisi prius*, and the Iudges of the circuit of that Countie in that vacation and meane time before the day of appearance appointed for the Iurie aboue, here by their Commission of *Nisi prius* haue authority to take the appearance of the Iury in the County before them, and there to heare the Witnesses & proofes on both sides concerning the issue of fact, and to take the verdict of the Iury, and against the day they should haue appeared aboue, to returne the verdict read in the Court aboue, which returne is called a *Postea*.

The manner of proceeding of Iustices of Circuits in their circuits.

The course the Iudges hold in their Circuits in the execution of their Commission concerning the taking of Nisi prius.

* Distringas.

Postea.

And

And vpon this verdict clearing the matter in Fact, one way or other, the Iudges aboue giue iudgement for the partie for whom the verdict is found, and for such damages and costs as the Iury doe assesse.

By those tryals called *Nisi prius*, the Iuries and the parties are eased much of the charge they should bee put to, by comming to London with their Euidences & Witnesses, and the Courts of Westminster are eased of much trouble they should haue, if all the Iuries for tryals should appeare and try their causes in those Courts; for those Courts aboue haue little leisure now; though the Iuries come not vp, yet in matters of great weight or where the title is intricate or difficult, the Iudges aboue, vpon information to them, doe retaine those causes to bee tryed there, and the Iuries doe at this day in such causes come to the Barre at *Westminster*.

The fift Commission that the Iudges in their Circuits doe sit by, is the Commission of the Peace in euery Countie of their circuit. And all the Iustices of the Peace hauing no lawfull impediment, are bound to be present at the Assizes to attend the Iudges, as occasion shall fall out: if any make default, the Iudges may set a fine vpon him at their pleasure and discretions. Also the Sheriffe in euery shire through the Circuit, is to attend in

5. Commission is a Commission of the Peace.

The Iustices of the Peace and the Sheriffe are to attend the Iudges in their Countie.

person, or by a sufficient deputie allowed by the Iudges, all that time they be within the Countie, and the Iudges may fine him if hee faile, or for negligence or misbehauiour in his Office before them; and the Iudges aboue may also fine the Sheriffe for not returning or not sufficient retourning of Writs before them.

Propertie in Lands, is gotten and transferred by one to another, by these foure manner of wayes.

1 By Entry.
2 By Discent.
3 By Escheat.
4 Most vsually by Conueyance.

Of propertie of Lands to be gained by Entrie.

1 Propertie by Entry is, where a man findeth a piece of Land that no other possesseth or hath title vnto, and hee that so findeth it doth enter, this Entry gaineth a Propertie; this Law seemeth to be deriued from this text, *Terra dedit filijs hominum*, which is to be vnderstood, to those that will till and manure it, and so make it yeeld fruit; and that is he that entreth into it, where no man had it before. But this manner of gaining Land

Lands was in the first dayes & is not now of vse in England, for that by the cōquest, all the Land of this Nation was in the Conquerours hands, & appropriated vnto him; except Religious and Church-lands, and the lands in Kent, which by composition were left to the former owners, as the Conquerour found them, so that no man but the Bishopricks, Churches, and the men of *Kent*, can at this day make any greater title then from the Conquest to any Lands in England; And Lands possessed without any such title, are in the Crowne, and not in him that first entreth; as it is by Land left by the Sea, this Land belongeth to the King and not to him that hath the Lands next adioyning, which was the ancient Sea Bankes; This is to bee vnderstood of the inheritance of Lands: viz. That the inheritance cannot bee gained by the first entry. But an estate for an other mans life by out-Lawes, may at this day be gotten by entrie. As a man called *A.* hauing land conueyed vnto him for the life of *B.* dyeth without making any estate of it, there, whosoeuer first entreth into the Land after the decease of *A.* getteth the propertie in the Land for time of the continuance of the estate which was granted to *A.* for the life of *B.* which *B.* yet liueth, and therefore the said Land cannot reuert till *B.* die. And to the heire of *A.* it cannot goe, for that

All Lands in England were the Conquerours and appropriated to him vpon the Conquest of England, and held of him, except 1. Religious and Church-lands. 2 The lands of the men of Kent.

Land left by the Sea belongeth to the King.

that it is not any state of inheritance, but only an estate for another mans life; which is not descendable to the heire, except he be specially named in the grant: viz. To him and his heirs. As for the Executors of A. they cannot haue it, for its not an estate testamentory, that it should goe to the Executors as goods and Chattels should, so as in truth no man can intitle himselfe vnto those Lands; and therefore the Law preferreth him that first entreth, and he is called *Occupans*, and shall hold it during the life of B. but must pay the rent, performe the conditions, and doe no wast. And he may by deed assigne it to whom he please in his life time. But if he die before he assigne it ouer, then it shall go againe to whomsoeuer first entreth and holdeth. And so all the life of B. so often as it shall happen.

Occupancie.

Likewise if any man doth wrongfully enter into another mans possession, and put the right owner of the freehold and inheritance from it, he therby getteth the freehold & inheritance by disceisin, & may hold it against all men, but him that hath right, & his heires, & is called a disseisor. Or if any one die seised of lands, and before his heire doth enter, one that hath no right doth enter into the Lands, and holdeth them from the right heire, hee is called an Abator, and is lawfull owner against all men, but the right heire.

And

And if such person Abator, or disseisor (so as the disseisor hath quiet possession fiue yeares next after the disseisin) doe continue their possession, and die seised, and the land discend to his heire, they haue gained the right to the possession of the Land against him that hath right till he recouer it by fit action reall at the common law. And if it be not sued for at the common law within threescore yeares after the disseisin, or abatement committed, The right owner hath lost his right by that negligence. And if a man hath diuers Children, and the elder being a Bastard doth enter into the land and enioyeth it quietly during his life, and dieth therof so seised, his heires shall hold the land against all the lawfull Children and their issues.

Propertie of Lands by discent.

Propertie of Lands by discent is, where a man hath Lands of inheritance and dyeth, not disposing of them, but leauing it to goe (as the Law casteth it) vpon the heire. This is called a discent of Law, and vpon whom the discent is to light, is the question. For which purpose the Law of inheritance preferreth the first Child before all others, and amongst childrē the male before the female; and amongst males the first borne. If there be no Children, then the Brother, if no Brothers, then sisters, if neither Brothers nor Sisters, then Vnckles, & for lacke of Vnckles Ants, if none of them, then Couzens in the neereſt degree of conſanguinity, with theſe three rules of diuerſities. 1. That the Eldeſt male ſhall ſolely inherit; but if it come to females, then they being all in an equall degree of neereneſſe ſhall inherit altogether, and are called Parceners, and all they make but one heire to the Anceſtor. 2. That no brother nor ſiſter of the halfe blood ſhall inherit to his brother or ſiſter, but as a Child to his Parents. as for example. If a man haue two wiues, and by either wife a ſonne, the eldeſt ſon ouerliuing his Father is to be preferred to the inheritance of the Father being Fee-ſimple; But if he entreth & dyeth without a child, the Brother ſhall not be his heire, becauſe he is of the halfe bloud to him, but the Vncle of the eldeſt Brother or Siſter of the whole bloud, yet if the eldeſt Brother had dyed or had not entred in the life of the Father, either by ſuch entry or conueiance, then the youngeſt Brother ſhould inherit the Land that the Father had, although it were a child by the ſecond wife, before any daughter by the firſt. The third rule about diſcents. That land purchaſed ſo by the partie himſelfe that dyeth, is to be inherited; firſt, by the heires of the Fathers ſide, then if he haue none of that part, by the heires of the Mothers ſide. But Land deſcended to him from his father or mother, are to goe to that ſide onely from which they came, and not to the other ſide.

[illegible]

Brother or ſiſter of the halfe bloud ſhall not inherit to his Brother or Siſter but only as a child to his Parents

Diſcent.

Thoſe

Thoſe Rules of diſcent mentioned before are to be vnderſtood of Fee-ſimples, and not of entailed Lands, and thoſe rules are reſtrained by ſome particular cuſtomes of ſome particular places: as namely, the cuſtome of *Kent*, that euery male of equall degree of Childhood, Brotherhood or kindred, ſhall inherit equally, as daughters ſhall being Parceners, and in many Borough Townes of England, and the Cuſtome alloweth the youngeſt ſonne to inherit, and ſo the youngeſt Daughter. The Cuſtome of *Kent* is called *Gauelkind*. The Cuſtome of Boroughes *Burgh Engliſh*.

Cuſtomes of certaine places

And there is another note to bee obſerued in Fee-ſimple inheritance, and that is, that euerie heire hauing fee-ſimple Land or inheritance, be it by common Law or by Cuſtome of either gauelkind or burgh Engliſh, is chargeable ſo farre forth as the value thereof extendeth with the binding acts of the Anceſtors from whom the inheritance deſcendeth; and theſe acts are colaterall encombrances, and the reaſon of this charge is, *Qui ſentit commodmu ſentire debet & incommodum ſiue onus*. As for example, if a man bind himſelſe and his heires in an obligation, or doe Couenant by writing for him and his heires, or do grant an Annuity for him & his heires, or do make a warranty of Land binding him and

Euery Heire hauing land is bound by the binding Acts of his inceſtors if hee bee named.

and his heyres to warrantie : in all these cases the Law chargeth the heyre after the death of the Ancestor with this obligation, Couenant, Annuity & Warrantie; yet with these three cautions: first, That the partie must by speciall name binde himselfe & his heires, or couenant, grant and warrant for himselfe and his heires; otherwise the heire is not to be touched. Secondly, That some action must bee brought against the heire whilest the land or other inheritance resteth in him vnaliened away: for if the Ancestor dye, & the heire, before an action be brought against him vpon those Bonds, Couenants, or Warranties doe alien away the land, then the heire is cleane discharged of the burthen, except the land was by fraud conveyed away, of purpose, to preuent the suit intended against him. Thirdly, that no heire is further to be charged than the value of the land descended vnto him from the same ancestor that made the Instrument of charge, and that land also, not to bee sold out-right for the debt, but to be kept in extent and at a yearely value, vntill the debt or damage bee run out. Neuerthelesse if an heire that is sued vpon such a debt of his ancestor doe not deale clearely with the Court when he is sued, that is, if he come not in immediately, & by way of confession set downe the true quantitie of his inheritance descended, and so submit him-

Dyer 114. Plowden.

Dyer 149. Plowden.

Dny & Pepps case.

himselfe therfore, as the Law requireth, then that heire that otherwise demeaneth himself, shall be charged of his owne other lands and goods, and of his money, for this Deed of his ancestor. As for example: If a man binde himselfe and his heires in an Obligation of one hundred pounds, and dyeth leauing but ten acres of land to his heire, if his heire bee sued vpon the Bond, and commeth in, and denieth that hee hath any lands by discent, and it is found against him by the verdict that he hath ten acres, this heire shall be now charged by his false plea of his owne lands, goods & body, to pay the hundred pound, although the ten acres be not worth ten pound.

Heire charged for his false plea.

Propertie of lands by Escheat, is where the owner dyed seised of the lands in possession without childe or other heyre, thereby the land for lacke of other heire is said to escheat to the Lord of whom it is holden. This lacke of heire happeneth principally in two cases: first, where the lands owner is a Bastard. secondly, where hee is attainted of Felonie or Treason. For neither can a Bastard haue anie heire except it bee his owne childe, nor a man attainted of Treason, although it be his owne childe.

Propertie of lands by Escheat.

Two causes of Escheat. 1. Bastardy. 2. Attainder of Treason, felonie.

Vpon attainder of Treason the King is to

Attainder of Treason entitleth the King, though the lands be not holden of him, otherwise in attainder of felonie &c. for there the King shall haue but *Annum diem & vastum.*

F haue

haue the land, although hee be not the Lord of whom it is held, because it is a royall Escheat. But for Felonie it is not so, for there the King is not to haue the Escheat, except the land be holden of him: and yet where the land is not holden of him, the King is to haue the land for a yeare and a day next ensuing the iudgement of the attainder, with a libertie to commit all maner of wast all that yeare in houses, gardens, ponds, lands and woods.

In Escheat two things are to be obserued. 1. The tenure. 2. The manner of the Attainder. All lands are holden of the Crowne immediatly or mediately by Mesne Lords, the Reason. Concerning the tenure of Lands.

In these Escheats, two things are especially to be obserued; the one is, the tenure of the lands, because it directeth the person to whom the Escheat belongeth, viz. the Lord of the Mannor of whom the Land is holden. 2. The manner of such attainder which draweth with it the Escheat. Concerning the Tenures of Lands, it is to be vnderstood, that all lands are holden of the Crowne either mediately or immediately, and that the Escheat appertaineth to the immediate Lord, and not to the mediate. The reason why all land, is holden of the Crowne immediatly or by Mesne Lords, is this.

The Conquerer by right of Conquest got all the Lands of the realme into his hands, and as hee gaue it he still reserued rents and seruices. Knights seruice in *Capite* first instituted.

The Conquerer got by right of Conquest all the land of the Realme into his owne hands in demeasne, taking from euery man all estate, Tenure, propertie and libertie of

the

the same, (except Religious and Church lands, and the Land in *Kent*) and still as hee gaue any of it out of his owne hand, he reserued some retribution of rents, or seruices, or both, to him and to his heires; which reseruation, is that, which is called the tenure of Land.

The reseruat i ons in Knights seruice tenure was 4.
1. Marriage of the Wards male and female.
2. Horse for seruice.
3. Homage and fealty.
4. Primer Seisin.

In which reseruation, hee had foure Institutions, exceeding politique and sutable to the state of a Conquerer.

The policie of the Conquerour in the reseruation of seruices constituted in foure particulars, was to haue the marriage of his Wards both Male and Female.

1 Seeing his people to be part *Normans*, and part *Saxons*, the *Normans* hee brought with him, the *Saxons* he found heere: he bent himselfe to conioyne them by marriages in amitie, and for that purpose ordaines, that if those of his nobles, Knights and Gentlemen, to whom hee gaue great rewards of Lands should dye, leauing their heire within age, a Male within 21. and a female within 14. yeares, and vnmarried, then the King should haue the bestowing of such heires in marriage in such family, and to such persons as he should thinke meete, which interest of marriage went still imployed, and doth at this day in euery tenure called Knigh ts seruice.

Interest of marriage goeth employed in euery tenure by Kinghts seruice.

Referuatioh that his tenant should keepe a horse of Seruice, and serue vpon him himselfe, when the king went to warres, which is a part of that seruice called Kinghts seruice.

The second was, to the end that his people should still bee conserued in warlike exercises and able for his defence; when therefore hee gaue any good Portion of Lands, that might make the partie of abilities or strength, hee withall reserued this seruice, That that partie and his heires hauing such Lands, should keepe a horse of seruice continually, and serue vpon him himselfe when the King went to wars, or else hauing impediment to excuse his owne person, should find an other to serue in his place; which seruice of horse and man, is a part of that tenure called Knights seruice at this day.

But if the Tenant himselfe bee an Infant, the King is to hold this Land himselfe vntill he come to full age, finding him meat, drinke, apparell, and other necessaries, and finding a horse anda man, with the ouerplus, to serue in the warresas the Tenant himself should do if he were at full age.

But if this inheritance descend vpon a woman, that cannot serue by her sex, then the King is not to haue the Lands, she being of 14. yeares of age, because shee is then able to haue an husband, that may do the seruice in person.

The

The third Institution, that vpon euery guift of Land the King reserued a vow and an Oath to bind the partie to his faith & loyaltie, that vow was called *Homage*, the oath *Fealtie*. Homage is to be done kneeling, holding his hands betweene the knees of the Lord, saying in the French tongue; I become your man of Life and limbe, and of earthly honour. Fealtie, is to take an oath vpon a booke, that hee will be a faithfull Tenant to the King, and doe his seruice, and pay his rents according to his tenure.

Ayd money to make the Kings eldest Son a Kinght, or to marry his eldest Daughter, is likewise due to his Maiestie from euery one of his Tenants in Knights seruice, that hold by a whole fee 20 s. and from euery Tenant in Soccage if his land be worth 20. pound *per ann*. 20. s. *vide* N. 3. fol. 82.

3. Institution of the Conquerour was, that his tenants by Knights seruice vow vnto loyaltie, which he called Homage, and make vnto him oath of his faith which was called Fealtie.
1. Homage.
2. Fealtie.

The fourth Institution, was that for Recognizon of the Kings bounty by euery heire succeding his ancestor in those Knights seruice lands, the King should haue *Primer seisin* of the lands, which is one yeares profit of the lands, and vntill this be paid the King is to haue possession of the land, and then to restore it to the heire; which continueth at this day in vse, and is the

Escuage was likewise due vnto the King from his Tenant by Knights seruice: when his Maiestie made a voyage royall to warre against another Nation, those of his Tenants that did not attend him there for 40. dayes with Horse and furniture fit for seruice, were to be assessed in a certaine summe by Act of Parliament, to bee payed vnto his Maiesty, which assessement is called Escuage.

4. Institution was for Recognizon of the Kings bounty, to be payd by euery heire vpon the death of his ancestor, which is one yeares profit of the Lands, called, *Primer seisin*.

the very cause of suing Liuerie, and that as well where the heire hath bin in ward as otherwise.

Knights Seruice in Capite, is a Tenure *de persona Regis.*

These before mentioned be the rights of the tenure, called Knights seruice in *Capite*, which is as much to say, as tenure *de persona Regis, & Caput*, being the chiefest part of the person, it is called a Tenure in *Capite*, or in Chiefe. And its also to be noted, that as this tenure in *Capite* by Knights seruice generally was a great safetie to the Crowne, so also the Conquerour instituted other tenures in Capite necessary to his estate; as namely, he gaue diuers lands to be holden of him by some speciall Seruice about his person, or by bearing some speciall Office in his house, or in the Field, which haue Knights seruice and more in them, And these hee called Tenures by *Grand Serieantie.* Also he prouided vpon the first gift of Lands, to haue Reuenues by continuall Seruice of Ploughing his Land, repairing his Houses, Parkes pales, Castles and the like. And sometimes to a yearely prouision of Gloues, Spurres, Hawkes, Horses, Hounds and the like; which kind of reseruations are called also tenures in Chiefe or in Capite of the King, but they are not by Knights seruice, because they required no personall seruice, but such things as the Tenants may hire another to doe

Tenants by Grand Serieantie, were to pay reliefe at the full age of euery heire, which was one yeeres value of the lands so held *vltra Repriss.*

Grand Serieantie.

Pettie Serieantie.

doe or prouide for his money. And this Tenure is called a tenure by Soccage in Capite, the word *Soccagium* signifying the Plough, howbeit in this later time, the Seruice of Ploughing the land is turned into mony rent, and so of Haruest workes, for that the Kings doe not keepe their Demeasne in their owne hands as they were wont to doe, yet what Lands were *De antiquo Dominico Corona*, it well appeareth in the Records of the Exchequer called the booke of Doomesday. And the Tenants by ancient Demeasne, haue many immunities & priuiledges at this day, that in ancient times were granted vnto those Tenants by the Crowne, the particulars whereof are too long to set downe.

The institution of Soccage in Capite, and what it is now turned into monies rents. Ancient Demeasne Tenure, what?

These Tenures in *Capite*, as well that by *Soccage*, as the others by *Knights seruice*, haue this propertie; that the Tenants cannot alien their Lands without licence of the King: if he do, the King is to haue a Fine for the contempt, and may seize the land, and retaine it vntill the fine be paid. And the reason is, because the King would haue a libertie in the choyce of his Tenant, so that no man should presume to enter into those Lands and hold them (for which the King was to haue those speciall seruices done him) without the Kings leaue; This licence and fine as it is now disgested is easie and of course.

There

Office of Alienation.

A licence of alienation is the third part of one yeeres value of the land moderately rated.

There is an office called the office of *Alienation*, where any man may haue a licence at a reasonable rate, that is, at the third part of one yeares value of the Land moderately rated. A Tenant in *Capite* by Knights seruice or grand Serieantie, was restrained by ancient Statute, that hee should not giue nor alien away more of his Lands, than that with the rest he might be able to doe the seruice due to the King; and this is now out of vse.

Aid a summe of mony ratably leuied according to the proportion of the lands.

Euery Tenant by Knights seruice in Capite, had to make the Kings eldest Son a Knight, or to marry his eldest daughter.

And to this Tenure by Knights Seruice in chiefe, was incident that the King should haue a certaine summe of money, called *Aid*; due to bee ratably leuied amongst all those Tenants proportionably to his Lands, to make his eldest Sonne a Knight, or to marry his eldest Daughter.

Tenants by Soccage in Cap. must sue liuerie and pay Primer Seisin, and not to bee in Ward for bodie or land.

And it is to bee noted, that all those that hold Lands by the Tenure of Soccage in *Capite* (although not by Knights seruice) cannot alien without licence, and they are to sue liuery, and pay Primer Seisin, but not to be in Ward for bodie or Land.

How Mannors were at first created.

Mannors created by great men in imitation of the policie of the king in the institutions of tenures.

By example and resemblance of the Kings policie in these Institutions of Tenures, the Great men and Gentlemen of this Realme

did

did the like so neere as they could; as for example, when the King had giuen to any of them two thousand Acres of Land, this party purposing in this place to make his dwelling, or (as the old word is) his Mansion house, or his Mannor house; did deuise how he might make his Land a compleat habitation to supply him with all manner of necessaries, and for that purpose, hee would giue of the outtermost parts of those two thousand Acres, 100. or 200. Acres, or more or lesse, as he should thinke meet, to one of his most trustie Seruants, with some reseruation of rent to find a horse for the Warres, and goe with him when hee went with the King to the Warres, adding vowe of Homage, and the Oath of Fealtie, Wardship, Marriage, and reliefe. This Reliefe is to pay fiue pound for euery Knights Fee, or after the rate for more or lesse at the entrance of euerie Heire; which Tenant so created and placed, was and is to this day called a Tenant by Knights Seruice, & not by his own persone, but of his Mannors; of these he might make as many as he would. Then this Lord would prouide that the Land which he was to keepe for his own vse, should be ploughed, & his Haruest brought home, his House repayred, his Parke pailed, and the like: and for that end he would

A manere, the word Manner.

Knights seruice tenure reserued to common persons.

Knights Seruice Tenure created by the Lord is not a Tenure by Knights seruice of the person of the Lord, but of his Mannor.

Reliefe is fiue pound to be paid by euery Tenant by Knights seruice to his Lord vpon his entrance respectiuely for euery Knights fee descended.

Soccage Tenure reserued by the Lord.

would giue some lesser parcels to sundry others, of twentie, thirtie, fortie or fiftie Acres; reseruing the seruice of ploughing a certaine quantitie, or so many dayes of his Land, and certaine Haruest workes or dayes in the Haruest to labour, or to repaire the House, Parke pale, or otherwise, or to giue him for his Prouision Capons, Hens, Pepper, Commin, Roses, Gilliflowers; Spurres, Gloues, or the like; or to pay him a certaine rent, and to be sworne to be his faithfull Tenant, which Tenure was called a soccage Tenure, & is so to this day, howbeit most of the ploughing and haruest seruices, are turned into mony rents.

Reliefe of Tenant in Soccage, one years rent and no wardship or other profit vpon the dying of the Tenant.

Ayd mony and Escuage mony is likewise due vnto the Lords of their Tenants, *vide* N. 3. fol. 82. and 83.

The Tenants in Soccage at the death of euery Tenant were to pay reliefe, which was not as Knights seruice is, fiue pound a Knights fee. But it was, and so is still, one yeares rent of the Land; and no wardship or other profit to the Lord. The remainder of the two thousand Acres he kept to himselfe, which he vsed to manure by his bondmen, and appointed them at the Courts of his Mannor how they should hold it, making an entrie of it into the Roll of the Remembrances of the Acts of his Court, yet still in the Lords power to take it away: and therefore

fore they were called Tenants at will, by Coppie of Court Roll; being in truth bondmen at the beginning, but hauing obtained freedome of their persons, and gained a custome by vse of occupying their Lands, they now are called Coppie-holders, and are so priuiledged, that the Lord cannot put them out, and all through Custome. Some Coppie-holders, are for liues, one, two, or three successiuely; & some inheritances from heire to heire by custome, and custome ruleth these estates wholly, both for widdowes estates, fines, harriots, forfeitures, and all other things.

Villenage or Tenure by Coppie of Court Roll.

Mannors being in this sort made at the first, reason was that the Lord of the Mannor should hold a Court, which is no more then to assemble his Tenants together, at a time by him to be appointed; in which Court, he was to be informed by oath of his Tenants, of all such duties, rents, reliefes, Wardships, Copie-holds or the like, that had hapned vnto him; which information is called a presentment, and then his Bailife to seize and distraine for those duties if they were denied or with holden, which is called a Court Baron, and herein a man may sue for any debt or Trespasse vnder 40[l] value, and the Freeholders are to iudge of the cause vpon proofe produced vpon both sides. And

Court Baron, with the vse of it.

Suit to the Court of the Lord incident to the Tenure of the Free-holders.

therfore the Free-holders of these Mannors, as incident to their Tenures, doe hold by suit of Court, which is to come to the Court, & there to iudge betweene partie and partie in those pettie actions, and also to informe the Lord of duties of rents and seruices vnpaid to him from his Tenants. By this course it is discerned who be the Lords of lands, such as if the Tenants dye without heire, or be attainted of felonie or Treason, shall haue the Land by Escheat.

What attainders shall giue the Escheat to the Lord. Attainders, 1. By iudgement, 2. By verdict or confession. 3. By outlawry, giue the Lands to the Lord.

Now concerning what attainders shall giue the Escheat to the Land, it is to be noted, that it must eyther bee by iudgement of Death giuen in some Court of Record against the Felon found guiltie by Verdict, or confession of the Felonie, or it must bee by Out-lawry of him.

Of an Attainder by Outlawrie.

The Out-lawrie groweth in this sort, a man is Indicted for Felonie, being not in hold, so as he cannot be brought in person to appeare & to be tryed, insomuch that Processe of *Capias* is therfore awarded to the Sheriffe, who not finding him returneth *Non est inventus in Balliva mea*; and thereupon another *Capias* is awarded to the Sheriffe, who likewise not finding him maketh the same returne, then a Writ called an *Exigent* is directed to the Sheriffe, commanding him to Proclaime

claime him in his Countie Court fiue feuerall Court dayes to yeeld his body, which if the Sheriffe doe, and the party yeeld not his body, he is sayd by the Default to be Out-lawed, the Coroners there adiudging him Out-lawed, and the Sheriffe making the returne of the Proclamations and of the iudgement of the Coroners vpon the backside of the writ. This is an attainder of Felonie, whereupon the Offender doth forfeit his Lands by an Escheat to the Lord of whom they are holden.

Prayer of Cleargie.

But note, that a man found guilty of Felonie by verdict or confession, and praying his Cleargie, and thereupon reading as a Clerke, and so burnt in the hand and discharged, is not attainted, because he by his Cleargy preuenteth the iudgement of death, and is called a Clerke conuict, who loseth not his Lands, but all his Goods, Chattels, Leases and Debts.

He that standeth mute forfeiteth no lands, except for Treason.

So a man indicted that will not answer nor put himselfe vpon tryall, although he be by this to haue iudgement of Pressing to Death, yet he doth forfeit no Lands, but Goods, Chattels, Leases and Debts, except his offence be Treason, and then he forfeiteth his Lands to the Crowne.

He that killeth himselfe forfeiteth but his Chattels.

So a man that killeth him-selfe shall not lose his Lands, but his Goods, Chattels, Leases and Debts. So of those that kill others in their owne defence, or by misfortune.

Flying for Felony, a forfeiture of Goods.

A man that beeing pursued for Felonie, and flyeth for it, loseth his Goods for his flying, although hee returne and is tryed, and found not guiltie of the Fact.

He that yeeldeth his body vpon the Exigent for Felonie forfeiteth his goods.

So a man Indicted of Felonie, if hee yeeld not his body to the Sheriffe vntill after the Exigent of Proclamation is awarded against him, this man doth forfeit all his goods for his long stay, although hee be found not guiltie of the Felonie, but none is attainted to lose his lands, but onely such as haue Iudgements of Death by tryall vpon verdict or their owne confession, or that they be by Iudgement of the Coroners out-lawed as before.

Lands entaild, Escheat to the King for Treason.

Besides the Escheats of lands to the Lords of whom they be holden for lacke of heires, and by attainder for Felony (which onely doe hold place in Fee-simple lands) there are also forfeiture of Lands to the Crowne by attainder of Treason; as namely, if one that hath entailed Lands commit Treason, he he forfeiteth the profits of the lands for his life to the Crowne, but not to the Lord.

Stat. 26. H. 8.

And if a man hauing an estate for life of himselfe or of another, commit Treason or Felonie, the whole estate is forfeited to the Crowne, but no Escheat to the Lord.

Tenant for life committeth Treason or Felony, there shal be no Escheat to the Lord.

But a Coppie-hold, for Fee-simple, or for life, is forfeited to the Lord and not to the Crowne; and if it be entailed, the Lord is to haue it during the life of the offender onely, and then his heire is to haue it.

The Custome of *Kent* is, that Gauilkind land is not forfeitable nor Escheatable for Felonie, for they haue an old saying; The Father to the Bough, & the Son to the plough.

If the Husband was attainted, the Wife was to lose her thirds in cases of Felonie and Treason, but yet she is no offender; but at this day it is holden by Statute Law that shee loseth them not, for the Husbands Felony. The relation of these forfeits are these.

The wife loseth no power notwithstanding the husband be attainted of Felonie.

Of the Relation of Attainders, as to the Forfeiture of Lands and goods with the diuersity.

1. That men attainted of Felonie or Treason by verdict or Confession, do forfeit all the Lands they had at the time of their offence committed, and the King or the Lord whosoeuer

Attainder in Felony or treason by verdict, confession, or outlawry, forfeiteth all they had from the time of the offence committed.

soeuer of them hath the Escheat or forfeiture, shall come in and auoid all Leases, Statutes, or conueyances done by the offender, at any time since the offence done. And so is the Law cleare also if a man bee attainted for Treason by outlawry; but vpon attainder of felonie by outlawry, it hath beene much doubted by the Law-bookes whether the Lords title by escheat shall relate backe to the time of the offence done, or onely to the date or teste of the writ of Exigent for Proclamation, whereupon he is outlawed; howbeit at this day it is ruled, that it shall reach backe to the time of his fact, but for goods, chattels, and debts, the Kings title shall looke no further backe then to those goods, the partie attainted by verdict or confession, had at the time of the verdict & confession giuen or made, And in outlawries at the time of the Exigent as well in Treasons as Felonies: wherein it is to be obserued, that vpon the parties first apprehension, the Kings Officers are to seize all the goods and Chattels, and preserue them together, dispending onely so much out of them as is fit for the sustentation of the person in prison, without any wasting, or disposing them vntill conuiction, and then the propertie of them is in the Crowne, and not before.

And so it is vpon an attainder of outlawry, otherwise it is in the attainder by verdict, confession and outlawrie, as to their relation for the forfeiture of goods and Chattels.

The Kings Officers vpon the apprehension of a Felon are to seize his goods and Chattels.

It

It is alſo to bee noted, that perſons attainted of Felonie or Treaſon, haue no capacitie in them to take, obtaine or purchaſe, ſaue onely to the vſe of the King, vntill the partie be pardoned. Yet the partie giueth not backe his Lands or Goods without a ſpeciall Patent of Reſtitution, which cannot reſtore the bloud without an Act of Parliament. So if a man haue a Sonne, and then is attainted of Felonie or Treaſon & pardoned, and purchaſeth Lands, and then hath iſſue another ſon, and dyeth; the Sonne he had before he had his pardon, although he be his eldeſt Sonne, and the Patent haue the words of reſtitution to his Lands, ſhall not inherit, but his ſecond Sonne ſhall inherit them, And not the firſt; becauſe the bloud is corrupted by the Attainder, and cannot be reſtored by Patent alone, but by Act of Parliament. And if a Man haue two Sonnes; and the eldeſt is attainted in the life of his Father, and dyeth without iſſue, the Father liuing, the ſecond ſonne ſhall inherit the Fathers Lands; but if the eldeſt Son haue any iſſue, though he die in the life of his Father, then neither the ſecond Son, nor the iſſue of the eldeſt, ſhall inherit the Fathers Lands, but the Father ſhall there be accompted to dye without Heire, & the Land ſhall Eſcheate, whether the eldeſt Sonne haue iſſue or not afterward or before, though he be pardoned after the death of his Father.

A perſon attainted may purchaſe, but it ſhall be to the Kings vſe. There can be no reſtitution in Bloud without Act of Parliament, but a pardon enableth a man to purchaſe, and the heire begotten after ſhall inherit thoſe Lands.

Propertie of Lands by Conueyance, is first distributed into estates, for Yeares, for Life, in Tayle, and Fee-simple.

Propertie of Land by conueyance diuided into. 1. Estates in Fees. 2. In Tayle. 3. For Life. 4. For Yeeres.

THese Estates are created by word, by writing, or by record. For Estates of Yeares, which are commonly called Leases for Yeares, they are thus made; where the owner of the Land agreeth with the other by word of mouth, that the other shall haue, hold, & enioy the Land, to take the profits therof for a time certaine of Yeares, Moneths, Weekes or Dayes, agreed betweene them; and this is called a lease Paroll; such a lease may be made by writing Pole or Indented of deuise grant and to farme let, and so also by fine of Record, but whether any Rent be reserued or no, it is not materiall. Vnto these leases there may bee annexed such exceptions, conditions and Couenants, as the parties can agree on. They are called Chattels Reall, and are not inheritable by the heires, but goe to the Executors and Administrators, and be saleable for debts in the life of the owner, or in the Executors or Administrators

Lease Paroll.

Lease by writing Pole or indented.

A rent need not to be reserued.

Lease for yeares they go to the Executors and not to the Heires.

Administrators hands by Writs of Execution vpon Statutes, Recognizances, Iudgements of Debts or Damages. They be also forfeitable to the Crowne by Outlawry, by Attainder for Treason, Felonie, or Premunire, killing himselfe, Flying for Felonie, although not guilty of the fact, standing out or refusing to be tryed by the Country, by Couiction of Felonie, by verdict without Iudgement, Pettie larcenie, or going beyond the Sea without licence.

By what meanes they are forfeitable.

Leases are to be forfeited by attainder. 1. In Treason. 2. Felonie. 3. Premunire. 4. By killing himselfe. 5. For flying. 6. Standing out or mute, or refusing to be tryed by the Country. 7. By Conuiction. 8. Pettie larcenie. 9. Going beyond the Sea without License.

They are forfeitable to the Crowne, in like manner as Leases for Yeares, or interest gotten in other mens Lands, by extending for debt vpon Iudgement in any Court of Record, Stat. Merchant, Stat. Staple, Recognizances, which being vpon Statutes are called Tenants by Stat. Merchant, or Staple, the other Tenants by Elegit, and by Wardship of Body and Lands, for all these are called Chattels Reall, and goe to the Executors and Administrators, and not to the heires, and are saleable and forfeitable as Leases for yeares are.

Extents vpon Stat. Staple. Marchant, Elegit, Wardship of Bodie and Lands are Chattels, and forfeitable in the same manner as leases for yeares are.

Lease for life is not forfeitable by outlawry except in cases of Felonie or Premunire, and then to the King and not to the Lord by Escheat; and it is not forfeited by any of the meanes before mentioned of leases for yeares.

What Liuery of Seisin is, and how it is requisite to euery Estate for life.

Leases for liues are also called Freeholds, they may also be made by Word or writing, there must be Liuerie and Seisin giuen at the making of the Lease, whom we call the Lessor; who commeth to the doore, backside or Garden if it be a house, if not, then to some part of the Land, and there he expresseth, that hee doth grant vnto the taker called the Lessee, for tearme of his life: and in Seisin thereof, hee deliuereth to him a Turfe, twig, or Ring of the doore; and if the Lease bee by writing, then commonly there is a note written on the backeside of the Lease, with the names of those witnesses who were present at the time of the Liuerie of Seisin made; This estate is not saleable by the Sheriffe for Debt, but the Land is to be extended for a yearely value, to satisfie the Debt. It is not forfeitable by Outlawrie, except in cases of Felonie, nor by any of the meanes before mentioned, of Leases for yeares; sauing in an Attainder for Felonie, Treason, Premunire, and then onely to the Crowne, and not to the Lords by Escheat.

Indorsement of Liuerie vpon the Backe of the deed and witnesse of it.

Lease for life not to be sould by the Sheriffe for debt but extended yeerly.

A man that hath bona Felon. by Charter, shall not haue the meanes if leaser for life bee attainted.

And though a Noble man or other, haue liberty by Charter, to haue all Felons Goods; yet

yet a Tenant holding for tearme of life, being attainted of Felonie, doth forfeit vnto the King and not to this Noble man.

Occupant.

If a man haue an Estate in Lands for another mans life, and dyeth; this Land cannot goe to his Heire, nor to his Executors, but to the partie that first entreth; and he is called an Occupant as before hath beene declared.

Of estate talies, and how such an estate may be limited

A Lease for yeares or for life may be made also by fine of Record, or bargaine and sale, or Couenant to stand seized vpon good considerations of Marriage, or Bloud, the reasons whereof, are hereafter expressed.

Entayles of Lands are created by a gift, with Liuerie and Seisin to a man, and to the heires of his body; this word (Body) making the entaile, may be demonstrated and restrained to the Males or Females, heires of their two bodies, or of the body of either of them, or of the body of the Grand father or father.

By the Stat. of West. 1. made in *E*. 1. time, estates in tayle were so strengthened they were not forfeitable by any attainder.

Entayles of Lands began by a Statute made in *Ed*. 1. time, by which also they are so much strengthened, as that the Tenant in Tayle could not put away the Land from the heire by any Act of conueyance or Attainder, nor let it, nor incumber it, longer then his own Life.

The great inconuenience that ensued thereof.

But the inconuenience thereof was great, for by that meanes, the Land being so sure tyed vpon the heire as that his Father could not put it from him, it made the Sonne to bee disobedient, negligent, and wastfull; often marrying without the Fathers consent, and to grow insolent in vice, knowing, that there could be no checke of dis-inheriting him. It also made the owners of the land lesse fearefull to commit Murthers, Felonies, Treasons, and Manslaughters; for that they knew, none of these acts could hurt the Heire of his inheritance. It hindred men that had intayled lands, that they could not make the best of their lands by fine and improuement, for that none vpon so vncertaine an estate as for terme of his own life would giue him a fine of any valew, nor lay any great stocke vpon the land that might yeeld rent improued.

The preiudice the Crowne receiued therby.

Lastly, those Entailes did defraud the Crowne, and many Subiects of their Debts; for that the land was not lyable longer then his owne life-time; which caused that the King could not safely commit any office of accompt to such, whose land were entailed, nor other men trust them with loane of money.

These

These inconueniences were all remedied by Acts of Parliament; as namely, by Acts of Parliament later then the Acts of Entailes, made, 4. *H*.7.32.*H*.8. A Tenant in taile may dis inherit his Sonne by a fine with Proclamation, and may by that meanes also, make it subiect to his Debts and Sales.

The Stat 4.*H*.7 and 32.*H*.8.to bar estates taile by fine.

By a Statute made, 26.*H*.8. A Tenant in taile doth forfeite his lands for Treason; and by an other Act of Parliament, 32. *H*.8. He may make leases good against his heire for 21. yeares, or three liues; so that it be not of his chiefe Houses, Lands, or demeasne, or any lease in Reuersion, nor lesse rent reserued then the Tenants haue payed most part of 21. yeares before, nor haue any manner of discharge for doing wasts and spoiles: by a Statute made 33. *H*.8. tenants of Entayled lands are lyable to the Kings debts by Extent, and by a Stat. made 13. & 39. *Eliz.* they are saleable for the arrerages vpon his accompt for his Office; So that now it resteth, that Entailed Lands haue two priuiledges only, which be these. First, not to be forfeited for Felonies. Secondly, not to bee extended for Debts after the parties death, except the Entailes be cut off by Fine and Recouerie.

26.*H*.8.

32.*H*.8.

33.*H*.8.

13.&.39.*Eliz*.

Entailes two priuiledges. First, Not forfeitable for Felonie. Secondly, Not extendable for the Debts of the partie after his death: *Prouiso*, not to put away the Land from his next heyre. If he doe, to forfeit his owne Estate, and that his next heyre must enter.

But

Of the new deuice called a Perpetuitie, which is an Entayle with an addition.

But it is be noted that since these notable Statutes, and remedies prouided by Statutes, doe dock Entayles, there is start vp a deuice called Perpetuitie, which is an Entayle with an addition of a *Prouiso* Conditionall, tyed to his Estate, not to put away the Land from his next heyre; and if he doe, to forfeit his owne estate. Which Perpetuities if they should stand, would bring in all the former inconueniences subiect to Entayles, that were cut off by the former mentioned Statutes, and farre greater; for by the Perpetuitie, if he that is in possession start away neuer so little, as in making a Lease, or selling a little quillet, forgetting after two or three Discents, as often they doe, how they are tyed, the next Heyre must enter; who peraduenture is his Sonne, his Brother, his Vncle or kinsman, and this raiseth vnkind Suites, setting all that kindred at iarres, some taking one part, some another, & the principal parties wasting their time and mony in suites of law. So that in the end, they are both constrained by necessitie to ioyne both in a Sale of the land, or a great part of it, to pay their Debts, occasioned through their Suites; And if the chiefest of the Family for any good purpose of well seating himselfe, by selling that which lyeth farre off is to buy that which is neere, or for the aduancement of his Daughters or younger Sonnes, should haue reasonable

These Perpetuities would bring in all the former inconueniencies of Estates tailes.

The inconueniencies of those Perpetuities.

ble cause to sell, this Perpetuitie, if it should hold good, restraineth him. And more then that where many are owners of inheritance of land not Entayled, may during the minoritie of his Eldest sonne, appoint the profits to goe to the aduancement of the younger Sons and Daughters, and pay Debts by Entayles and Perpetuities: the owners of these lands cannot doe it, but they must suffer the whole to discend to his eldest Sonne, and so to come to the Crowne by Wardship all the time of his Infancie.

Wherefore seeing the dangerous times and vntowardly Heyres, they might preuent those mischiefes of vndoing their Houses by conueying the Land from such heyres, if they were not tyed to the stake by those Perpetuities, and restrained from Forfeiting to the Crowne, and disposing of it to their owne or to their Childrens good; Therefore it is worthy of consideration, whether it be better for the Subiect and Soueraigne to haue the lands secured to mens Names & Blouds by perpetuities, with all inconueniences aboue-mentioned, or to be in hazzard of vndoing his House by vnthriftie posteritie.

Quere whether it be better to restraine men by these Perpetuities from alienations, or to hazard the vndoing of houses by vnthrifty Posteritie.

The last and greatest Estate of Lands is Fee-simple, and beyond this there is none of the former for Liues, Yeares or Entayles; but

The last and greatest Estate in Land is Fee-simple.

but beyond them is Fee simple. For it is the greatest, last and vttermost degree of Estates in Land; therefore hee that maketh a Lease for life, or a gift in tayle, may appoint a remainder when he maketh another for life or in tayle, or to a third in Fee-simple; but after a Fee-simple hecan limit no other estate. And if a man doe not dispose of the Fee-simple by way of remainder, when he maketh the gift in tayle, or for liues, then the Fee-simple resteth in himselfe as a Reuersion. The difference between a Reuersion & a Remainder, is this. The Remainder is alwayes a succeeding Estate, appointed vpon the gifts of a precedent Estate, at the time when the Precedent is appointed. But the Reuersion is an estate left in the giuer, after a particular estate made by him for Yeares, Life, or Entaile; where the remainder is made with the particular estates, then it must bee done by Deeds in writing, with Liuerie and Seisin, and cannot be by words; And if the giuer will dispose of the Reuersion after it remaineth in himselfe, he is to doe it by writing, and not by word; and the Tenant is to haue notice of it, and to atturne it, which is to giue his assent by word or paying rent, or the like; and except the Tenant will thus atturne, the partie to whom the Reuersion is granted cannot haue the Reuersion, neither can he compell him by any Law to atturne, except the grant of the Re-

uersion

A remainder cannot be limitted vpon an estate in Fee-simple.

The difference betweene a remainder and a Reuersion.

A Reuersion cannot bee granted by word.

Atturnement must be had to the grant of the Reuersion.

The tenant not compellable to atturne but where the Reuersion is granted by fine.

uersion be by fine; and then hee may by writ prouided for that purpose: and if he doe not purchase that writ, yet by the fine, the Reuersion shall passe; and the Tenant shall pay no rent, except he will himselfe, nor be punished for any wastes in houses, woods &c. vnlesse it be granted by bargaine and Sale by Indenture inrolled; These Fee-simple estates lye open to all perrils of Forfeitures, Extents, Incumbrances and sales.

What a Feofment of land is.

Lands may be conueyed six manner of wayes.
1 By Feofment.
2 By Fine.
3 By Recouery
4 By Vse.
5 By Couenant
6 By Will.

Lands are conueyed by these 6. means; First, by Feofment, which is, where by Deed Lands are giuen to one and his heires, and Liuerie and Seisin made according to the forme and effect of the deed; if a lesser estate then Fee-simple bee giuen, and liuerie of seisin made, it is not called a Feofment, except the Fee-simple be conueyed, but is otherwise called a lease for life or gift intaile as aboue mentioned.

What a Fine is, and how lands may be conueied hereby.

A Fine is a reall agreement, beginning thus, *Hæc est finalis Concordia, &c.* This is done before the Kings Iudges in the Court of Common Pleas, concerning lands that a man should haue from another to him and his Heires, or to him for his Life, or to him and the heires males of his body, or for yeares certaine, whereupon rent may bee reserued, but no Condition or Couenants. This Fine is a Record of great credit, and vpon this Fine are foure Proclamations made openly in the Common Pleas; that is, in euery Terme one for foure Termes together; and if any man hauing right to the same, make not his claime within fiue yeares after the Proclamations ended, he loseth his right for euer, except hee be an Infant, a Woman couert, a Mad-man, or beyond the Seas, and then his right is saued; so that hee claime within fiue yeares after the death of her husbands full age, recouerie of his wits, or returne from beyond the Seas. This Fine is called a Feofment of Record, because that it includeth all that the Feofment doth, and worketh further of his own nature, & barreth Intailes peremptorily, whether the heire doth clayme within fiue yeares or not, if he claime by him that leuied the Fine.

Fine yeares non Clayme barreth not.
1 An Infant.
2 Feme Couert
3 Mad-man.
4 Beyond Sea.

Fine is a Feofment of Record.

Recoueries are where for assurances of lands the parties doe agree, that one shall begin an Action reall against the other, as though he had good right to the land, and the other shall not enter into Defence against it, but alleadge that hee bought the land of *I.H.* who had warranted vnto him, and pray that *I.H.* may bee called in to defend the Title, which *I.H.* is one of the Cryers of the Common Pleas, & is called the *Common Voucher*. This *I.H.* shall appeare and make as if he would

What Recoueries are.

Common Voucher one of the Criers of the Court.

would defend it, but shall a pray day to be assigned him in his matter of Defence; which being granted him at the Day, hee maketh Default, and thereupon the Court is to giue iudgement against him; which cannot be for him to lose his lands because he hath it not, but the partie that he hath sold it to, hath that who vouched him to warrant it.

Therefore the Demandant who hath no defence made against it, must haue Iudgement to haue the land against him that hee sued (who is called the Tenant) and the Tenant is to haue Iudgement against *I.H.* to recouer in value so much Land of his, where in truth he hath none, nor neuer will. And by this Deuice grounded vpon the strict Principles of Law, the first Tenant loseth the land, and hath nothing for it; but it is by his owne agreement for assurance to him that bought it.

Iudgement for the Demaundant against the Tenant in taile.

Iudgement for the Tenant to recouer so much land in value of the Common voucher.

This Recouerie barreth Entayles, and all Remainders and reuersions that should take place after the Entayles, sauing where the king is giuer of the Entayle and keepeth the Reuersion to himselfe; then neither the Heire, nor the Remainder, nor Reuersion, is barred by the recouerie

A recouery barreth an Eschear taile and all reuersions and remaindments thereupon.

The reason why a Common Recouery barreth those in Remainder & Reuersions.

The reason why the Heires, Remainders, and Reuersions are thus barred, is because in strict Law the recompence adiudged against the Gryer that was Vouchee, is to goe in succession of Estate as the Land should haue done, and then it was not reason to allow the Heire the libertie to keepe the Land it selfe, and also to haue recompence; and therefore he loseth the Land, and is to trust to the Recompence.

The many inconueniencies of estates in tayle brought in these Recoueries, which are made now common conueyances and assurances for Land.

This sleight was first inuented, when Entayles fell out to be so inconuenient as is before declared, so that men made no Conscience to cut them off, if they could finde Law for it. And now by vse, those Recoueries are become common assurances against Entailes, Remainders, and Reuersions, and are the greatest security Purchasers haue for their monies; for a Fine will barre the Heire in tayle, and not the Remainder, nor Reuersion, but a common Recouery will barre them all.

Vpon Fines, Feofments, & Recoueries, the estate doth settle according to the intent of the parties.

Vpon Feofments and Recoueries, the estate doth settle as the vse and intent of the parties is declared by word or writing, before the Act was done; As for example. If they make a writing, that one of them shall leuie a Fine, make a Feofment, or suffer a common Recouerie to the other; but the vse and

and intent is, that one ſhould haue it for his life, and after his deceaſe, a ſtranger to haue it in Tayle, and then a third in Fee-ſimple. In this caſe the land ſetleth in an eſtate according to the vſe & intent declared. And that by reaſon of the Statute made 27. HENRY 8. conueying the Land in poſſeſſion to him that hath intereſt in the vſe, or intent of the Fine, Feofment, or Recouerie, according to the vſe and intent of the parties.

Vpon this Statute is likewiſe grounded the forth and fifth of the ſix Conueyances, *viz.* Bargaines, Sales, Couenants, to ſtand ſeized to vſes; For this Statute, whereſoeuer it findeth an vſe, conioyneth the poſſeſſion to it, and turneth it into like quality of Eſtate, Condition, Rent and the like, as the vſe hath.

Bargaines, Sales and Couenants to ſtand ſeized to a vſe, are all grounded vpon one Statute

The vſe is but the equity and Honeſtie to hold the Land *in Conſcientiâ boni viri*. As for example. I and you agree that I ſhall giue you money for your Land, and you ſhall make me aſſurance of it. I pay you the money, but you made me no aſſurance of it. Here although the eſtate of the Land bee ſtill in you, yet the equitie and Honeſtie to haue it is with me; and this equity is called the Vſe, vpon which I had no remedy but in Chancerie,

What a vſe is.

Before 27.*H*.8. there was no remedie for a vse, but in Chancerie.

Chancerie, vntill this Statute was made of 27, *Henry*. 8. and now this Statute conioyneth and containeth the Land to him that hath the vse. I for my money paid to you, haue the Land it selfe, without any other Conueyance from you; and it is called a Bargaine and Sale.

The Stat. of 27.*H*.8. doth not passe Land vpon the payment of mony without a deed indented and Enrolled.

But the Parliament that made that Statute did foresee, that it would be mischieuous that mens Lands should so sodainly vpon the paiment of a little money be conuayed from them, peraduenture in an Alehouse or a Tauerne vpon straineable aduantages, did therefore grauely prouide an other Act in the same Parliament, that the Land vpon payment of this money should not passe away, except there were a Writing Indented, made betweene the said two Parties, and the said Writing also within six Moneths Inrolled in some of the Courts at Westminster, or in the Sessions Rolles in the Shire where the land lyeth; vnlesse it be in Cities or Corporate Townes where they did vse to Enroll Deeds, and there the Statute extendeth not.

The Stat of 27. of *H* 8. extendeth not into Cities and Corporate Townes where they did vse to Enroll Deeds.

A conueyance to stand seized to a vse.

The fifth Conueyance of a Fine, is a Conueyance to stand seized to vses: it is in this sort; A man that hath a Wife and Children, Brethren and kinsfolkes, may by writing vnder

vnder his Hand and Seale, agree, that for their or any of their preferment hee will stand seized of his Lands to their vses, either for life in tayle or Fee, so as he shall see cause; vpon which agreement in Writing, there ariseth an Equitie or Honestie, that the land should goe according to those agreements; Nature and Reason allowing these prouisions; which Equitie and Honestie is the vse. And the vse being created in this sort, the Statute of 27. *Henry* the Eight before mentioned, conueyeth the Estate of the land, as the vse is appointed.

Vpon an agreement in writing to stand seized to the vse of any of his kindred, a vse may be created, and the estate of the land thereupon executed by 27. *H.* 8.

And so this Couenant to stand seized to vses, is at this day since the said Statute, a Conueyance of land, and with this difference from a Bargaine and sale; in that this needeth no Enrollment as a Bargaine and Sale doth, nor needeth it to be in writing Indented, as Bargaine and Sale must: and if the partie to whose vse he agreeth to stand seized of the land, be not Wife, or Child, Couzen, or one that he meaneth to marry, then will no vse rise, and so no Conueyance; for although the Law alloweth such weightie Considerations of Marriage and bloud to raise vses, yet doth it not admit so trifling Considerations, as of Acquittance, Schooling, Seruices, or the like.

A Couenant to stand seized to a vse needeth no Enrolment as a Bargaine and Sale to a vse doth, so it be to the vse of Wife, Child, or Cozen, or one hee meaneth to marry.

Vpon a Fine, Feofment or Recouerie a man may limit the vſe to whom he liſteth, without Conſideration of bloud, or money. Otherwiſe, in a Bargaine and Sale, or Couenant.

But where a man maketh an eſtate of his land to others, by Fine, Feofment or Recouery, he may then appoint the vſe to whom hee liſteth, without reſpect of Marriage, kindred, or other things; for in that caſe his owne Will and declaration guideth the equity of the Eſtate. It is not ſo when hee maketh no eſtate, but agreeth to ſtand ſeized, nor when he hath taken any thing, as in the caſes of Bargaine, and ſale, and Couenant, to ſtand to vſes.

Of the continuance of land by will.

The laſt of the ſix Conueyances, is a Will in writing; which courſe of Conueyance was firſt ordained by a Statute made 32. *H*. 8. before which Statute no man might giue land by will, except it were in a Borrough-Town, where there was an eſpeciall cuſtome that Men might giue their lands by will; as in London, and many other places.

The not diſpoſing of Lands by will, was thought to bee a defect at the Common Law.

The not giuing of Land by Will, was thought to bee a defect at Common Law, that men in the wars, or ſuddainely falling ſicke, had not power to diſpoſe of their lands, except they could make a Feofment, or leuie a Fine, or ſuffer a Recouery; which lacke of time would not permit: and for men to doe it by theſe meanes, when they could not vndoe it againe, was hard; beſides, euen to the laſt houre of death, mens minds might alter

vpon

vpon further proofes of their Children or Kindred, or encreaſe of Children or debt, or defect of ſeruants or friends, to be altered.

For which cauſe, it was reaſon that the Law ſhould permit him to reſerue to the laſt inſtant the diſpoſing of his lands, and to giue him meanes to diſpoſe it, which ſeeing it did not fitly ſerue, men vſed this deuiſe.

The Court that was inuented before the Stat. of 32. *H.* the 8. firſt gaue power to deuiſe Lands by Will, which was a Conueyance of Lands to Feoffeers in truſt, to ſuch perſons as they ſhould declare in their Will.

They conueyed their full eſtates of their lands in their good health, to friends in truſt, properly called Feoffees in truſt; and then they would by their wils declare how their Friends ſhould diſpoſe of their lands; & if thoſe Friends would not performe it, the Court of Chancery was to compell them, by reaſon of the truſt; & this truſt was called, the vſe of the land, ſo as the Feoffees had the land and the party himſelfe had the vſe, which vſe was in equity, to take the profits for himſelfe, & that the feoffees ſhould make ſuch an eſtate as he ſhould appoint them; and if he appointed none, then the vſe ſhould goe to the heire, as the eſtate it ſelfe of the land ſhould haue done; for the vſe was to the Eſtate like a ſhadow following the body.

The inconueniences of putting Land into vſe.

By this courſe of putting lands into vſe, there were many Inconueniences,(as this vſe which grew firſt for a reaſonable cauſe,)*viz.* To giue men power and libertie to diſpoſe of their owne, was turned to deceiue many of their iuſt and reaſonable rights; As namely, a man that had cauſe to ſue for his land, knew not againſt whom to bring his action, nor who was owner of it. The wife was defrauded of her thirds. The Husband of being Tenant by curteſie. The Lord of his Wardſhip, Reliefe, Heriot, and Eſcheat. The Creditor of his Extent for debt. The poore Tenant of his leaſe; for theſe rights and duties were giuen by Law from him that was owner of the land, and none other; which was now the Feoffee of truſt, and ſo the old owner which wee call the Feoffor ſhould take the profits, and leaue the power to diſpoſe of the land at his diſcretion to the Feoffee, and yet he was not ſuch a Tenant as to bee ſeized of the land, ſo as his Wife could haue Dower, or the lands bee extended for his Debts, or that he could forfeit it for Felonie or Treaſon, or that his Heire could be Ward for it, or any duty of Tenure fall to the Lord by his Death, or that he could make any leaſes of it.

The frauds of conueiances to vſe by degrees of time, as they encreaſed, were remedied by the Statutes.

Which frauds by degrees of time as they encreaſed, were remedied by diuers Statutes; as

namely,

1.H.8. 4.H.8. 1.R.3. 4.H.7. 16.H.8. Stat. binding Cestuy que vse.

namely, by a Statute of the 1.*Henry*,6. and 4.*Henry*,8. it was appointed that the action may bee tryed against him which taketh the profits, which was then *Cestuy que vse* by a Statute made 1.*Richard*,3. Leases and Estates made by *Cestuy que vse* are made good, & Estat. by him acknowledged. 4 *Henry*,7. the Heire of *Cestuy que vse* is to be in Ward: 16.*Henry*, 8. the Lord is to haue reliefe vpon the death of any *Cestuy que vse*.

27.H.8. taking away all vses reduceth the Law to the ancient forme of Conueyances of Land, by Feofment, Fine, and Recouerie.

Which frauds neuerthelesse multiplying daily, in the end 27. *Henry*,8. the Parliament purposing to take away all those vses, and reducing the Law to the ancient forme of conueying of Lands by publike Liuery of Seisin, Fine, and Lecouerie; did ordaine, that where lands were put in trust or vse, there the possession and estate should be presently carryed out of the Friends in trust, and settled and inuested on him that had the Vses, for such tearme and Time as he had the Vse.

In what manner the Stat. of 32.H.8. giueth power to dispose of Lands by will.

By this Statute of 27.*Henry*,8. the power of disposing lands by Will, is cleareIy taken away amongst those frauds; whereupon 32. *Henry*, 8. another Statute was made, to giue men power to giue Lands by Will in this sort. First, it must be by Will in writing. Secondly, hee must be seized of an Estate in

 Fee-simple

Fee-simple; For Tenant for an other mans Life, or Terme in Tayle, cannot giue Land by Will, by that Statute 3. he must be solely seized, & not ioyntly with another; and then beeing thus seized, for all the Land he holdeth in Soccage Tenure, hee may giue it by Will, except he hold any peece of land in *Capite* by Knights seruice of the King: and then laying all his lackes together, hee can giue but two parts by Will; for the third part of the whole, as well in Soccage as in *Capite*, must descend to the Heire, to answer Wardship, Liuerie and primer Seisin, to the Crowne.

If a Man be seized of *Capite* Lands and Soccage, he cannot deuise but two parts of the whole.

The third part must descend to the Heire to answer Guardship, Liuerie and Seisin to the Crowne.

And so if he hold lands by Knights seruice of a Subiect, he can deuise of the land but two parts, and the third the Lord by Wardship, and the Heire by descent is to hold.

A Conueiance by deuise of *Capite* Lands to the Wife for her Ioynture, or to his Children for their good, or to pay Debts is void for a third part, by 32. *H*.8.

And if a man that hath three Acres of Land holden in *Capite* by Knights seruice, doe make a ioynture to his Wife of one, and conuey an other to any of his Children, or to Friends, to take the profits, and to pay his Debts or Legacies, or Daughters Portions, then the third Acre or any part thereof he cannot giue by Will, but must suffer it to descend to the Heire, and that must satisfie Wardship.

Yet

Yet a Man hauing three Acres as before, may conuey all to his Wife or Children by Conueyance in his Life time, as by Feofment, Fine, Recouerie, Bargaine and sale, or Couenant to stand seized to vses and to dis-inherit the Heire. But if the heire be within age when his Father dyeth, the King or other Lord shall haue that Heire in Ward, and shall haue one of the three Acres during the Wardship, and to sue Liuerie and Seisin. But at full age the Heire shall haue no part of it, but it shal go according to the Conueyance made by the Father.

But a Conueyance by Act executed in the life-time of the partie of such Lands to such vses is not void, but a third part: but if the heire be within age, he shall haue one of the Acres to be in Ward.

Afflictis afflictione addere.

It hath beene debated how the thirds shall be set forth. For it is the vse that all Lands which the Father leaueth to descend to the Heire, beeing Fee-simple, or in tayle, must be part of the thirds; and if it be a full third, then the King, nor Heire, nor Lord, can intermeddle with the rest; If it be not a full third, yet they must take it so much as it is, and haue a supply out of the rest.

Entailed lands part of the thirds.

The King nor Lord cannot intermeddle if a full third part be left to descend to the Heire.

This supply is to be taken thus; If it be the Kings Ward, then by a Commission out of the Court of Wards, whereupon a Iury by oath, must set forth so much as shall make vp the thirds, except the Officers of the Court of Wards can otherwise agree with the parties.

The manner of making supply when the part of the heire is not a full third.

parties. If there be no Wardship due to the King, then the other Lord is to haue this supply by a Commission out of the Chancerie, and Iury thereupon.

The Statutes giue power to the Testator to set out the third himselfe, and if it be not a third part, yet the King or Lord must take that in part, and haue a supply out of the Rent.

But in all those cases the Statutes doe giue power to him that maketh the Will to set forth and appoint of himselfe, which Lands shall goe for thirds, and neither King nor Lord can refuse it. And if it be not enough, yet they must take that in part, and only haue a supply in manner as before is mentioned out of the rest.

Propertie in Goods.

Of the seuerall wayes whereby a man may get Propertie in Goods or Chattels.

1. By Gift.
2. By Sale.
3. By Stealing.
4. By Wayuing.
5. By Straying.
6. By Shipwracke.
7. By Forfeiture.
8. By Executorship.
9. By Administration.
10. By Legacie.

1. Proper-

1. *Propertie by gift*

BY gift the property of goods may be passed by word or writing; but if there be a generall Deed of Gift made of all his Goods, this is suspitious to be done vpon fraud, to deceiue the Creditors.

A deed of gift of goods to deceiue his Creditors is void against them, but good against the Executors Administrators, or Vender of the partie himselfe.

And if a man who is in Debt, make a Deed of gift of all his Goods to protract the taking of them in Execution for his debt, this Deed of Gift is void, as against those to whom he stood indebted; but as against himselfe, his owne Executors or Administrators, or any man to whom afterwards he shall sell or Conuey them, it is good.

2. *By Sale.*

PRopertie in Goods by Sale. By Sale any man may conuey his owne Goods to another; and although he may feare Execution for Debts, yet he may sell them out-right for money at any time before the Execution serued, so that there be no reseruation of trust be-

What is a Sale *bona fide* and what not, when there is a priuate reseruation of trust betweene the parties.

tweene them, paying the money, he shall haue the goods againe; for that trust in such case, doth proue plainely a fraud to preuent the Creditors from taking the goods in Execution.

---

3. *By Theft or taking in Iest.*

How a Sale in Market shall be a barre to the owner.

PRopertie of Goods by Theft or taking in Iest. If any Man steale my Goods or Chattels, or take them from me in Iest, or borrow them of me, or as a Trespasser or Felon carry them to the Market or Faire, and sell them, this Sale doth barre me of the propertie of my goods, sauing that if hee be a horse he must be ridden two houres in the Market or Faire, betweene ten and fiue a clocke, and Tolled for in the Toll-Booke, & the seller must bring one to auouch his sale, knowne to the Toll-booke-keeper, or else the sale bindeth me not. And for any other goods, where the Sale in a Market or faire shal barre the owner being not the seller of his Propertie, it must be sale in a Market or Faire where vsuall things of that Nature are sold. As for example: if a man steale a Horse, & sell him in Smithfield, the true owner is barred by this Sale; but if he sell the Horse in Cheapeside, Newgate

Of Markets and what Markets such a Sale ought to be made in.

Newgate or Westminster market, the true owner is not barred by this Sale; because these Markets are vsuall for Flesh, Fish, &c. and not for Horses.

So wheras by the Custom of *London* euery Shop there is a Market all the dayes of the weeke, sauing Sundayes and Holydayes; Yet if a peece of Plate or Iewell that is lost, or Chaine of Gold or Pearle that is stolne or borrowed, be sold in a Drapers or Scriueners shop, or any others but a Goldsmith, this sale barreth not the true owner, *Et sic in similibus*.

Yet by stealing alone of Goods, the Thiefe getteth not such propertie, but that the owner may Seize them againe wheresoeuer he findeth them; except they were sold in Faire or Market, after they were stolne; and that *bona fide* without fraud.

The owner may Seize his goods after they are stolne

But if the Thiefe be condemned of the Felonie, or outlawed for the same, or outlawed in any personall Action, or haue committed a forfeiture of Goods to the Crowne, then the true owner is without remedie.

If the Thiefe be condemned for Felonie, or outlawed, or forfeit the stolne goods to the Crowne, the owner is without remedie.

Neuerthelesse if fresh after the goods were stolne, the true owner maketh pursuit after the Thiefe and goods, and taketh the Goods

But if he make fresh pursuit he may take his goods from the thiefe.

with the Thiefe, hee may take them againe; And if he make no fresh pursuit, yet if he prosecute the Felon, so farre as Iustice requireth, that is, to haue him Arraigned, Indicted, and found guilty (though hee be not hanged, nor haue Iudgement of Death) or haue him outlawd vpon the indictment; in all these cases he shall haue his goods againe, by a writ of Restitution to the partie in whose hands they are.

Or if he prosecuted the law against the Thiefe and conuict him of the same Felonie, he shall haue his goods againe by a writ of Restitution.

4. *By wayuing of Goods.*

BY Wayuing of Goods, a propertie is gotten thus. A Thiefe hauing stolne goods, being pursued flyeth away and leaueth the goods. This leauing is called Wayuing, and the propertie is in the King; except the Lord of the Mannor haue right to it, by Custome or Charter.

But if the Felon be Indicted, adiudged, or found guiltie, or outlawed at the suit of the Owner of these goods, he shall haue Restitution of these goods, as before.

5. *By Straying.*

BY Straying, propertie in liue Cattell is thus gotten. When they come into other mens,

mens grounds ſtraying from the owners, then the partie or Lord into whoſe grounds or Mannors they come, cauſeth them to be ſeized, and a With put about their neckes, and to be cryed in three Markets adioyning, ſhewing the markes of the Cattell; which done, if the true owner claymeth them not within a yeare and a day, then the propertie of them is in the Lord of the Mannor whereunto they did ſtray, if he haue all ſtrayes by Cuſtome or Charter, elſe to the King.

---

6. *Wracke, and when it ſhall be ſaid to bee.*

BY Shipwracke, property of Goods is thus gotten. When a Ship loaden is caſt away vpon the Coaſts, ſo that no liuing Creature that was in it when it began to ſinke eſcapeth to Land with life, then all thoſe Goods are ſaid to be wracked, and they belong to the Crowne if they be found; except the Lord of the Soyle adioyning can intitle himſelfe vnto them by Cuſtome, or by the Kings Charter.

---

7. *Forfeitures.*

BY Forfeitures, Goods and Chattels are thus gotten. If the Owner be outlawed, if he be indicted of Felonie, or Treason, or either confesse it, or be found guilty of it, or refuse to be tryed by Peeres or Iury, or be attainted by Iudgement, or flye for Felony; although he be not guilty, or suffer the Exigent to goe foorth against him; although he be not outlawed, or that he go ouer the Seas without license, all the goods hee had at the Iudgement, hee forfeiteth to the Crowne; except some Lord by Charter can claime them. For in those cases prescripts will not serue, except it be so ancient, that it hath had allowance before the Iustices in Eyre in their Circuits, or in the Kings Bench in ancient time.

8. *By Executorship.*

BY Executorship goods are gotten. When a man possessed of Goods maketh his Last Will and Testament in writing or by Word, and maketh one or more Executors thereof; These Executors haue by the Will and death of the parties, all the propertie of their Goods, Chattels, Leases for Yeares, Wardships and Extents, and all right concerning those things.

Those

Those Executors may meddle with the Goods, and dispose them before they proue the Will, but they cannot bring an action for any Debt or duety before they haue proued the Will.

Executors may before *probat* dispose of the goods, but not bring an action for any debt.

The prouing of the Will is thus. They are to exhibite the Will into the Bishops Court, and there they are to bring the witnesses, and there they are to be sworne, and the Bishops Officers are to keepe the Will Originall, and certifie the Copie thereof in Parchment vnder the Bishops Seale of Office, which Parchment so sealed, is called the Will proued.

What *probat* of the Will is, and in what manner it is made.

---

9. By Letters of Administration.

BY Letters of Administration propertie in goods is thus gotten. When a man possessed of goods dyeth without any Will, there such goods as the Executors should haue had if he had made a Will, were by ancient Law to come to the Bishop of the Diocesse, to dispose for the good of his soule that dyed, he first paying his Funerals and Debts, and giuing the rest *Ad pios vsus*.

Pÿ Vsus.

This is now altered by Statute Lawes, so as the Bishops are to grant Letters of Administration

nistration of the goods at this day to the Wife if shee require it, or Children, or next of kin; If they refuse it, as often they doe, because the debts are greater then the estate will beare, then some Creditor or some other will take it as the Bishops Officers shall thinke meet. It groweth often in question what Bishop shall haue the right of prouing Wills, & granting Administration of goods.

Where the Intestate had *Bona notabilia* in diuers Diocesses, then the Archbishop of that Prouince where he dyed is to commit the Administration.

In which Controuersie the rule is thus, That if the partie dead had at the time of his Death *Bona notabilia* in diuers Diocesses of some reasonable value, then the Arch-bishop of the Prouince where he dyed is to haue the probat of his Will, and to grant the Administration of his goods as the case falleth out; otherwise, the Bishop of the Diocesse where he dyed is to doe it.

Executor may refuse before the Bishop, if he haue not intermedled the goods.

If there be but one Executor made, yet he may refuse the Executorship comming before the Bishop, so that hee hath not entermedled with any of the goods before, or with receiuing Debts, or paying Legacies.

Executor ought to pay, 1 Iudgements. 2 Stat. Recogn: 3 Debts by bonds and bills sealed. 4 Rent vnpayed. 5 Seruants wages. 6 Head workmen 7 Shop-booke and Contracts by word.

And if there be more Executors then one, so many as list may refuse; and if any one take it vpon him, the rest that did once refuse may when they will take it vpon them, and no Executor shall bee further charged with

Debts

Debts or Legacies, then the value of the goods come to his hands; So that he fore-see that he pay Debts vpon Record, first debts to the King, then vpon Iudgements, Statutes, Recognizances, then Debts by Bond and Bill sealed, Rent vnpayed, Seruants wages payment to head workmen and lastly, Shop-bookes, and contracts by Word. For if an Executor, or Administrator pay debts to others before to the King, or debts due by Bond before those due by Record, or debts by Shop-bookes and Contracts before those by Bond, arrerages of Rent, and Seruants or work mens wages, he shall pay the same ouer againe to those others in the sayd degrees.

Debts due in equall degree of Record, the Executor may pay which of them he please before suit commenced.

But yet the Law giueth them choyce, that where diuers haue Debts due in equall degree of Record or specialty, hee may pay which of them hee will, before any suite brought against him; but if suite be brought he must pay them that get Iudgement against him.

Any one Executor may doe as much as all together, but if a debt be released and Assets wanting, he shall only be discharged.

Any one Executor may conuey the Goods, or release Debts without his companion, and any one by himselfe may doe as much as all together; but one mans releasing of Debts or selling of Goods, shall not charge the other to pay so much of the Goods, if there be not enough to pay debts; but it shall charge the

M party

party himselfe that did so release or conuey.

Otherwise of Administrators.

But it is not so with Administrators, for they haue but one authoritie giuen them by the Bishop ouer the goods, which authoritie being giuen to many is to be executed by all of them ioyned together.

Executor dieth making his Executor, the second Executor shall be Executor to the first Testator.

And if an Executor dye making an Executor, the second Executor is Executor to the first Testator.

But otherwise, if the Administrator die making his Executor, or if Administration be committed of his goods. In both cases, the Ordinarie shall commit Administration of the goods of the first Intestate.

But if an Administrator die intestate, then his Administrator shall not bee Executor or Administrator to the first; But in that Case the Bishop, whom we call the Ordinary, is to commit the Administration of the first Testators goods to his Wife, or next of kinne, as if hee had dyed intestate; Alwayes prouided, that that which the Executor did in his life-time, is to bee allowed for good. And so if an Administrator dye and make his Executor, the Executor of the Administrator shall not bee Executor to the first intestate; But the Ordinarie must new commit the Administration of the goods of the first Intestate againe.

Executors or Administrators may retaine.

If the Executor or Administrator pay Debts, or Funerals, or Legacies of his owne money, he may retaine so much of the goods in kind, of the Testator or intestate, and

shall

ſhall haue propertie of it in kind.

---

10. *Propertie by Legacie.*

PRopertie by Legacie, is where a man maketh a Will and Executors, and giueth Legacies, he or they to whom the Legacies are giuen muſt haue the aſſent of the Executors or one of them to haue his Legacie, and the propertie of that Leaſe or other goods bequeathed vnto him, is ſayd to bee in him; but hee may not enter nor take his Legacie without the aſſent of the Executors or one of them; becauſe the Executors are charged to to pay Debts before Legacies. And if one of them aſſent to pay Legacies, hee ſhall pay the value thereof of his owne purſe, if there bee not otherwiſe ſufficient to pay debts.

Executors or Adminiſtrators may retaine; becauſe the Executors are charged to pay ſome debts before Legacies.

But this is to be vnderſtood, by debts of Record to the King, or by Bill and Bond ſealed, or arrerages of Rent, or Seruants or Workmens wages; and not debts of Shopbookes, or Bills vnſealed, or Contract by word; for before them Legacies are to bee payed.

Legacies are to be payed before debts by Shopbookes, Bils vnſealed, or Contracts by word.

And if the Executors doubt that they ſhall not haue enough to pay euery Legacie, they may pay which they liſt firſt; but they may not ſell any ſpeciall Legacie which they will

Executor may pay which Legacie he will firſt.

If the Executors doe want they may sell any Legacie to pay Debts.

to pay Debts, or a Lease of goods to pay a money Legacie. But they may sell any Legacie which they wil to pay Debts, if they haue not enough besides.

When a Will is made and no Executor named, Administration is to be committed *Cum testamento annexo.*

If a man make a Will and make no Executors, or if the Executors refuse, the Ordinarie is to commit Administration *Cum Testamento annexo*, and take bonds of the Administators to perfome the Will, and hee is to doe it in such sort, as the Executor should haue done if he had beene named.

FINIS.

www.ingramcontent.com/pod-product-compliance
Lightning Source LLC
Chambersburg PA
CBHW021430180326
41458CB00001B/209
9781584772484